I0798821

The Original Church

The Original Church

What It Meant *and* STILL MEANS to Be a Christian

JAMES L. PAPANDREA

Scepter

Copyright © 2025 James L. Papandrea

The total or partial reproduction of this book is not permitted, nor its informatic treatment, or the transmission of any form or by any means, including electronic, mechanic, photocopy, or other methods without the prior written permission of the owners of the copyright.

Quotations from early Christian documents are either adaptations of the translations found in the Ante-Nicene and Nicene Fathers series or are the author's own translations or both. Quotations from Scripture, unless otherwise noted, are from the New Revised Standard Version, Catholic edition, or are the author's own translation.

Published by Scepter Publishers, Inc.
info@scepterpublishers.org
www.scepterpublishers.org
800-322-8773
New York

All rights reserved.

Cover art: Ancient Fayum portraits of Christians, third and fourth centuries. Public Domain.
Cover design: Marc Whitaker, MTW Design
Text design and pagination: Studio Red Design

Library of Congress Control Number: 2025933661

ISBN Paperback: 978-1-59417-573-2
ISBN Ebook: 978-1-59417-574-9

Printed in the United States of America

To the family that God has given me,
our home, a cell in the Body of Christ,
of which I am the husband and father,
and our household, House Papandrea,
of which I am a son.

Contents

CHAPTER ONE

Who Is the Original Church?

I wish I knew what *Christianity was.*

–Charles Reding[1]

When I was growing up in a Protestant denomination, the Protestants told me two things that have stuck with me my whole life. One of these things is true; the other is a lie. The one that's true—and make no mistake, I've based my entire career on the fact that it is true—is that Christians today should care what the earliest Christians believed and how they lived their faith. There should be a certain priority given to the early Church, as the expression of Christianity that is most authentic, because it is closest in time to Jesus and the apostles. Therefore, we as Christians should want to know how the earliest of our ancestors in the Faith interpreted the revelation of God in the Old Testament, in the incarnation of Jesus Christ, and in the New Testament.

1. John Henry Newman, *Loss and Gain: The Story of a Convert* (Longmans and Green, 1903), p. 294.

And we should want to imitate the earliest Christians in the ways in which they applied these interpretations to everyday life in the world.

Now, this doesn't mean that we have to agree with everything that all of the Church Fathers said, or everything they wrote in their thousands of commentaries on Scripture. And it certainly doesn't mean that we should try to recreate something gleaned and scraped together from the Book of Acts. The so-called "Acts chapter two church" or "Acts chapter four church" didn't even last until the end of the Book of Acts. And this is at least partly because the gospel had to spread beyond Jerusalem. No, we do recognize that our faith, and even our doctrines, develop over time. That is, through the writings of the apologists, who were trying to explain Christianity to non-Christians, and the writings of the theologians, who were trying to warn Christians against heresy, our doctrines were clarified and refined. To name just one example, we can see in the pages of the New Testament that even the apostles could not imagine a world without slavery, and it was not until the third century that Christian theologians began condemning the institution of slavery as inconsistent with the dignity of every human being made in the image of God. So, development is a good thing, and our attention to the early Church does not mean that we need to live in the past. But it does mean that it matters how the Christians of the first several centuries in the history of the

Church taught and lived the Faith, because in doing that, they were literally defining what Christianity *is* for us.

The other thing the Protestants told me was not true—it was a lie. Or, to be fair, we should call it a myth, since the very sincere and well-meaning Lutherans who told me this myth did not think they were lying to me. They believed it. This is what I call the myth of "pre-Catholic Christianity." I was told in my Protestant catechism classes, as I and my fellow junior-highers prepared for our confirmation, that the Protestant Reformation was about getting rid of all of the things the Catholic Church had added to the Faith, in order to get back to an original form of Christianity, a supposed pristine form, before it was ruined by the additions of superstitions and man-made traditions. At the time, it seemed to make sense to me, and I believed it. In fact, I believed both of these things to such an extent that, fifteen years later when I entered my PhD program, I was determined to study for myself what this "Original Church" looked like.

You already know where that road leads, and you know that I was certainly not the first person to take that journey, through the early Church, and eventually across the Tiber. And that's because, when I studied the early Church for myself, I found that there is no such thing as "pre-Catholic Christianity," and that the Original Church was the Catholic Church. Or at least it could be said that the Catholic Church is, and has always been throughout the centuries, the most authentic expression of original Christianity, and the most faithful lived experience to this thing that Jesus himself founded and called his *Church*. As St. John Henry Newman wrote, "As far as historical records go, Christianity and Catholicism are synonymous."[2]

MYTH
The Protestant Reformation was a reset back to an original form of Christianity.

TRUTH
The Protestant Reformation stripped away many elements of original Christianity that have always been part of the Faith, even including some of the books of the Old Testament.

2. Newman, p. 205.

We Have Found the Truth

The Christians . . . having gone and made a search, have found the truth. And as we have learned from their writings, they have come nearer to truth and genuine knowledge than anyone else. For they know and trust in God, the Creator of heaven and of earth, in whom and from whom are all things.

–Aristides, *Apology*, 15

Perhaps we should take a step back and ask, What is a *church*? The truth is, we don't really know what Jesus called it, since there are only two times in the Gospels where Jesus utters the word *church*: in Matthew 16:18, "You are Peter, and on this rock I will build my church," and Matthew 18:15, "If another member of the church sins against you . . . ". The Greek word there is *ekklesia*, but Jesus was most likely speaking Aramaic. So what Aramaic word was translated by Matthew into the word that we translate into English as *church*? Nobody knows. We only know it wasn't the word *synagogue*, because that would have been translated as, well, *synagogue*. And it seems pretty clear that what Jesus founded was going to be more of a continuation of the temple rather than the synagogue. Indeed, the temple would soon be destroyed, and the Church would pick up the baton of temple worship, complete with tabernacle and sacrifice (though now the unbloody kind), whereas the synagogue would go on as the post-temple expression of non-Christian Judaism and give birth to the rabbis and their expression of the ancient faith. And so, if we are to understand what Jesus meant by *church* and what he intended it to be, we have to rely on the writings of his disciples, the apostles. I think it's fair to assume that we can trust that they understood correctly what Jesus had intended, and that they passed this on to their disciples, who became the first bishops. But this is not a book on ecclesiology, per se—for the purposes of this book, I want to look at how the earliest *lay* Christians understood themselves as *members* of this thing called the Church.

It is often said that the birthday of the Church was on that first Pentecost, when Jesus kept his promise to send the Holy Spirit. Of course, this is not wrong, but I would like to propose another way of looking at it. I would like to propose that the birth of the Church was really "on the night when he was betrayed." In other words, on that Holy Thursday, at the Last Supper, when Jesus instituted the sacrament of the Eucharist, the Church was born. I suppose that then his passion and resurrection would be the baptism of the Church, and Pentecost would be the Church's confirmation. That's how I look at it, anyway. But the point is that Jesus founded the Church, not simply by teaching things (important as that is), but by the institution of *sacraments* that were always meant to be repeated, down through the centuries, as the Church waits for Christ to return. And it is through those sacraments that the earliest Christians defined not only the Church itself but also themselves as Christians.

There is a lot of talk about identity these days. *How do you identify?* The very question seems strange when we think about it. It has enormous implications for a person's self-awareness, even though nowadays it is often answered with a set of pronouns that are defined according to idiosyncrasies completely divorced from their actual grammatical significances. That is, *gender* is a grammatical term that has nothing to do with biological sex, and the proof of this is that inanimate objects have a gender in other languages—so, in Italy, cars are feminine, for example, and yet we all know that cars are not females. The point is, people have been conditioned to believe that they can create their own definition, even in opposition to reality, and even to the point of making themselves so unique that they have no one with whom to be in solidarity, except others who are only like them in that they, too, claim to be unique. Be that as it may, humans do have a natural need to make sense of who they are and to define themselves in ways that make them a part of something greater than themselves.

In the ancient world, identity was usually not something one could see on the surface. It had nothing to do with skin color, for example. Not that Roman culture didn't have racism—it did—but "race" was defined by where you were from and by what you sounded like when you talked. To speak Greek or Latin well was to be civilized. To speak with a thick accent, or to speak another language, was to be a foreigner, or worse, a barbarian, and to be looked down upon and discriminated against. Women, too, were often seen as second-class citizens, and of course slaves were not really considered people at all, at least not in the legal sense of having rights. And yet, the early Christians didn't care about any of those distinctions. They took St. Paul at his word, that "There is no longer Jew or Greek, there is no longer slave or free, there is no longer male and female, for all of you are one in Christ Jesus. And if you belong to Christ, then you are Abraham's offspring, heirs according to the promise" (Gal 3:28–29). To be sure, the early Christians did self-identify as members of something greater than themselves, something that made them different from the rest of the world. They were, more than any other identifier, members of this thing called the Church. But what did that *mean* to them? That's what this book is about. And I believe that we should want to know what it meant to them, because that's what it should also mean to us.

We Are the Soul of the World

For Christians are not distinguished from other people by country, language, or the customs which they observe. . . . To sum it all up in a word, what the soul is in the body, that's what the Christians are in the world.

–"Mathetes," *Epistle to Diognetus*, 5–6

To belong to the Church was to be a part of a group of people with a radically different worldview from the society around them. For example, Roman culture assumed that people were born into a certain station in life or that fate determined where you ended up, and whether you were born into money or taken into slavery, that was how it was supposed to be. Most people were meant to serve and entertain a few people (the very wealthy, or so-called one percent, was probably more like three percent in ancient Rome).

But the Christian believed that all people were really in the same situation. On the one hand, Christians believed something that would have seemed crazy to their pagan neighbors: that all people are created equal, with the dignity that comes from being created in the image of God, stamped with God's own imprint. On the other hand, all people are also created to be servants—that is, servants of God and of each other. Roman culture operated on the assumption that some were destined by the gods to be the aristocrats, and the others (most people) were meant to serve them. Christians believed that all people were children of the Most High, and yet all people were meant to serve.

Roman culture further assumed that the 97 percent who were meant to serve and entertain were not only of lesser value, but they were expendable. Their very lives were disposable. Slaves were considered property, always to be sexually available to their owners and subject to beatings, torture, murder, or just abandonment to homelessness and hunger at any time; and baby girls were considered a burden and useless, often thrown out on the garbage heap minutes after birth, to die of exposure or more likely to be raised by a pimp, to look forward to a life of slavery and prostitution. But the Christian believed that a slave could be a bishop, like Onesimus, or possibly even Pope St. Clement; and a woman could be a consecrated bride of Christ, with an important ministry of prayer and visitation, or a patron of the Church, the host of a congregation, or even the founder and spiritual mother of a monastic community. And women, just as much as men, could face death with courage and strength.

For the early Christians, the absolute equality of all people was taken for granted. But this idea, especially to say that slave and free were equals, was perhaps the most offensive to the Romans. To them it seemed antisocial, anarchist, treasonous, unpatriotic, subversive. Tertullian wrote, "The outcry is that the empire is filled with Christians—that they are in the fields, in the cities, and in the islands. They [the pagans] lament, as if it some calamity, that both sexes, all ages, and every class, even the highest ranks, are passing over to the profession of the Christian faith" (*Apology*, 1).

And so, the Christians were persecuted, tortured, and executed—really just for the crime of calling themselves Christians—and though the legal charges ranged from arson to atheism, the real issue was that the pagans were afraid of them. They were afraid that if Christianity grew, their Roman way of life and their worldview would not last. And that fear was not unfounded. But what the pagan Romans lamented as a calamity the Christians saw as a correction. They would be the soul of the world, perhaps even the conscience of the world, calling it to a higher purpose and a holier morality.

We Look for a Kingdom

And when you hear that we look for a Kingdom, you suppose, without making any inquiry, that we speak of a human kingdom. On the contrary, we speak of the Kingdom of God, as is evident from the confessions of their faith made by those who are charged with being Christians, even though they know that death is the punishment awarded to anyone who so confesses.

–St. Justin Martyr, *First Apology*, 11

To be clear, the early Christians did not see it as their mission to build the kingdom of God on earth. The kingdom is not something to be created by people; rather it has always been understood to be something that already exists, though not yet fully revealed—something that we hope for in the future yet try to live as though we're already in it. The earliest Christians lived according to the values of one kingdom, while living as strangers in another kingdom (or empire), one which feared them, and hated them, and tried to exterminate them.

Or at least it seemed like that some of the time. At other times, Christians lived peacefully with their non-Christian neighbors, working alongside them, and trying to figure out—one day at a time—what it meant to be "in the world, but not of the world." In the rest of this book, I want to explore how the earliest Christians lived, worked, and thought of themselves in the midst of a culture that, at best, didn't understand them and, at worst, thought them to be dangerous. Specifically, we're talking about the regular folks, not the bishops or famous theologians; not the leaders and teachers, but the lay Christians. This book is for lay Christians, so I hope to illuminate the everyday lives of the lay Christians of the Original Church, to see how we might learn from them and imitate them.

In the interest of full disclosure, I have to admit that this is a tricky task, because these everyday lay Christians didn't leave us a written record of their thoughts and feelings. They weren't trying to be famous, and so they weren't. They didn't blog, post their lunches on social media, or even keep journals, for the most part. They were anonymous, and they were fine with that. Even the few diaries of lay Christians that we have, such as the diary of St. Perpetua, or the pilgrimage itinerary of Egeria, are focused on important but unique moments in their lives. For Perpetua, it was her imprisonment leading up to her death. For Egeria, it was her pilgrimage to the Holy Land. But what about the regular workaday life of the average Christian in the early Church? For that, we have to glean what we can from the sources we have, such as the writings of the apologists, who were trying to explain Christianity to non-Christians (including Roman emperors). For the most part, we can assume that the apologists would not misrepresent the beliefs and behaviors of the early Christians, since their non-Christian audience would notice that kind of hypocrisy, and it would have undermined their arguments (which amounted to a plea for the cessation of persecution).

We have the writings of the other Church Fathers as well, but in all these we have to carefully cross-reference the sources, because sometimes when the Church Fathers are admonishing and encouraging the faithful, their explanations of what Christians do (and don't do) can be more like their wish list for how things *should* be rather than a description of how things actually were. Therefore, understanding the earliest Christians is not as simple as quoting the Church Fathers (especially if those quotations are taken out of context). Often, we can hear the advice that the bishops give their people, but we have to dig deeper to see whether we can know the extent to which that advice was followed. For example, we have many treatises and sermons from the Church Fathers about how Christians do not attend the Roman games and shows. And yet those treatises and sermons would not exist if no Christian ever attended the "spectacles." In truth, this seems to have been an ongoing struggle, part of the bigger question of how to discern which activities were acceptable for Christians and which ones were not.

And so, I've been studying, and teaching, and writing about the Original Church and the earliest Christians for thirty years now. I feel like I know them. In fact, they brought me back to the Catholic Church of my baptism and my Italian ancestry. In this book, I hope to introduce you to them through the many "*We are*" statements that I've taken from the early apologists. I encourage you to read the documents from which they come for yourself, but you can trust that I haven't taken them out of context so as to misrepresent the meaning.

In describing who the early Christians were, we hear them also in some ways telling us who we are, or at least, who we should be, if we are going to be faithful to the ideals of the Church that Jesus founded. In describing how they lived, they are also giving us a road map to our own lives and to the sanctification of our homes, our jobs, and, in short, the sanctification of ordinary life in the world. We are all called to holiness, and yet we are convinced that we do not have to be in any particular occupation or life situation to pursue holiness. In other words, you can sanctify the life that you already have—you don't need to start by living a different life, only perhaps by living your life a bit differently. And the lives of the everyday saints of the early Church, as different as their situation was, can be a guide for us.

This is not a book of apologetics, though at times it might feel like it is, because Western culture is now so heavily influenced by the Protestant Reformation, and so many Christians live as though the myth of "pre-Catholic Christianity" is true. Sometimes we can even see the influence of a Protestant mindset in American Catholicism, and so I will point out some of these problematic assumptions (busting the Protestant myths) along the way. I will sometimes speak of the Protestant point of view in very general terms, which does not do justice to the fact that there are many (in fact, tens of thousands) of Protestant denominations, and they do not all have the same beliefs. Much of what I will critique as part of the overall Protestant myth is typical of American fundamentalism, and in comparison, even the original Reformers such as Martin Luther would look positively Catholic next to them. Nevertheless, this is not a book about Protestantism, and so we won't take the time to cover the nuances of the different Protestant viewpoints. Naturally there will be exceptions to everything I will say about Protestantism in general, so consider my comments and comparisons to be a kind of "If the shoe fits . . . " situation.

I Am a Christian

I said, "Father, do you see—let us say—that this vessel lying here is a little pitcher, or is it something else?" And he said, "I see that it is." And I replied to him, "Can it be called by any other name than what it is?" And he said, "No." "Neither can I call myself anything else than what I am, a Christian."

–St. Vibia Perpetua

So, who is the Original Church? Notice that the question is not, *What* is the Original Church? The Church is not really a *what* so much as a *who*. The Original Church is the earliest Christians, living in close proximity to the time of the apostles and learning from leaders who had been disciples of the apostles and of their disciples. And for the earliest Christians, their identity, above anything else, was their membership in the Church. It's who they were and it's how they lived.

Having said that, we can see from the early sources that the earliest Christians thought of their identity as Christians in four categories, or perhaps another way to think of it is as four layers. And these will give us the themes for the following chapters. Specifically, for the early Christians of the Original Church, to be a Christian meant being part of an extended family (*we live as a family*); it meant being the people who gather at the table of the Eucharist and who believed what they had been taught (*we receive these things*); it meant having a God-defined morality that set them apart from their neighbors (*we share our food but not our wives*); and it meant the dignity and sanctification of work for the benefit of others (*we work for your benefit*). Finally, we'll conclude with what is not really a category of early Christian identity, but what was a reality of the marginalization experienced by the earliest Christians. This is both the reality that the early Christians were ridiculed (*we are laughed at*), and that their neighbors marveled at the fact that they were ready to die for this thing to which they belonged.

CHAPTER TWO

We Live as a Family

We who once hated and destroyed one another, and because of our different customs would not share the same hearth with people of a different tribe, now, since the coming of Christ, live as a family with them.

–St. Justin Martyr, *First Apology*, 14

The apostle John wrote that whoever would receive Christ would be adopted into the family of God (Jn 1:12–13). And although Jesus spoke of bringing a kingdom of God (or kingdom of heaven), and there are other important ways in which to understand the Church, such as the Bride of Christ (Eph 5) and the Body of Christ (1 Cor: 12), the regular Christians of the early centuries seem to have thought of the Church mostly as a family. In the Original Church, to become a member of the Church was to join a new family—in fact, a family that takes precedence over all previous families and loyalties (see Mt 10:37; Lk 14:26).

To enter the family of the Church meant that one now shared with Jesus the ability to call God *Father* (Jn 20:17). And getting a new Father meant one also got a new mother. John himself stood in for the rest of us at the foot of the Cross, when Jesus referred to his own mother, Our Lady, and said to John, "Here is your Mother" (Jn 19:27). So, when a person accepts and identifies with Christ, then Christ's Father becomes his Father, and Christ's mother becomes his mother. And we know this is true because that same apostle John would write about her in the Book of Revelation. In symbolic language, he would write of Satan's attempt to kill her son. And when that failed, John tells us, the devil set out against "the rest of her children" (Rv 12:17), which, given the fact that she had no other biological children, the Church Fathers interpreted as a reference to the Church and the persecution of the early Christians. In other words, *we* are Mary's other children.

MYTH
Mary had other biological children after Jesus.

TRUTH
The Church has always taught the perpetual virginity of Our Lady. The only debate in the early Church was whether the "brothers and sisters" of the Lord mentioned in the Gospels were stepsiblings or cousins.

The myth of "pre-Catholic Christianity" would have you believe that devotion to Our Lady was a later development, or worse, a corruption, of original Christianity. But that's simply not true. We have a document from the second century, known as the *Protevangelion of James*, which contains evidence of Marian devotion as well as the seeds of virtually all the Marian doctrines, including her perpetual virginity. What's remarkable about this is not so much the presence of Marian devotion in this early document, but the fact that the author of the document did not feel the need to argue for, or defend, these doctrines. They are simply assumed, and the document proposes to explain the historical background behind them.

Now, in the interest of full disclosure, the *Protevangelion* is pseudonymous—it wasn't really written by any of the New Testament Jameses, and so the document itself is not necessarily authoritative. But that, too, is significant, since it shows that devotion to Our Lady as Mother of God and the Mother of the Church was not something that was first formulated as a set of doctrines and then taught to the laity. It was always part of the devotion of the laity, coming from the grassroots of the Church—the original *sensus fidelium*, you might say. And we can see in the writings of the Church Fathers that the consensus among bishops and theologians of the early Church was that Mother Mary was immaculately conceived, was without sin, remained a virgin her whole life, and at her death was assumed into heaven as the first follower of Christ to experience the resurrection (the rest of us have to wait until his return for that; see below). The Church Fathers didn't all agree on who the "brothers and sisters of the Lord" in the Gospels are, but they all agreed they could not be biological children of Mary. In fact, even the original Protestant Reformers believed in the perpetual virginity of Mary—it was only later Protestants who began to deny it.

It goes without saying that we cannot do justice to the Blessed Virgin and Marian doctrine here. The point for the moment is to emphasize that for the original Christians, Jesus's Father was their Father, and Jesus's mother was their mother. From there, the Church itself was understood to be an extension of that family of God.

MYTH
Devotion to the Blessed Virgin was a later corruption of original Christianity.

TRUTH
Devotion to the Blessed Virgin was a part of the Christian faith from the beginning.

We Regard Each Other as Brothers and Sisters

According to age, we recognize some as sons and daughters, we regard others as brothers and sisters, and to the more advanced in life we give the honor due to fathers and mothers.

–Athenagoras, *A Plea for the Christians*, 32

It is sometimes said that the hierarchy of the Church developed in imitation of the Roman military, or Roman social class structure. But none of that is true. The structure of the Church was always organized like a family. But it did, to a certain extent, look like the Roman family. In Roman culture, the family was more than one household. As long as the oldest male member of an extended family remained alive, the ties of all of his offspring, both to him and to each other, were very strong. The patriarch of the extended family was called the *paterfamilias*, the "family father," and as long as he lived, even his sons didn't really own anything. He had authority over them and their families. Under Roman law, a *paterfamilias* could not only arrange a marriage for his sons and daughters, he could initiate a divorce for them if he found a more financially advantageous match later.

Of course, the Church never approved of Roman attitudes toward divorce, but the Church did inherit these strong family ties and connections. You might think of the

Christians in a particular city as an extended family, with the bishop as their *paterfamilias* and the individual house-congregations in that city as distinct households within the extended family. The pastors of the individual congregations were like the sons of the *paterfamilias*, each having authority over his own household, but under the authority of the patriarch. And this is why, to this day, we call our priests "father." If we didn't think it too lacking in formality, we might call our bishops "grandfather."

Jesus may have said, "Call no one your father" (Mt 23:9), but it's clear that everyone in the Original Church interpreted that statement as hyperbole, not to be taken literally, because they *did* call people father. It's safe to assume they didn't stop calling their own dads father, but in addition to that, St. Paul refers to himself as the father of those whom he converted to the Faith (Phlm 10), and even the pagans knew that Christians called their bishops their fathers, as we can see in documents like the *Martyrdom of Polycarp* (ch. 12) and St. Ignatius of Antioch's *Letter to Smyrna* (ch. 8). And there is no document from the early Church in which anyone objects to the practice. And so, the Church was a family, with priests as the fathers of households, bishops as patriarchs of the extended family in each city, and the bishop of Rome as the living representative of that ancestral father, or Papa, St. Peter.

MYTH
The hierarchy of the Church was patterned after Roman social or military hierarchies.

TRUTH
The Church was always structured like a family, with the bishop as the father of the extended family and the priest as the father of the household congregation.

This is just one part of the reason why the priesthood was reserved for men, so in case it needs to be said, those women who are mentioned in the New Testament as having the church meeting in their homes were not presiding over the sacraments there. Women such as Lydia or Priscilla would have been the *hosts* of a house-congregation, and as such they would have had a role as *patrons* of the Church, as part of the Roman patron-client system, but they would not have been considered pastors, since that required presiding over the sacraments, leading prayer, and teaching, and that authority went to the "father" of the house.

Also it should be clear that whereas a patron, or host, of a congregation would have had to be wealthy enough to own or rent the space for worship, the clergy of the Original Church were not necessarily wealthy or powerful. They were chosen to be the fathers of their congregations not because they had any power in society, but because they were the disciples of the previous generation of leaders. And even a slave could be a bishop.

MYTH
There were female clergy in the early Church.

TRUTH
There were women who were wealthy patrons of the Church and who hosted congregations in their homes, but there is no evidence that women ever presided over the sacraments. The priests and bishops were the fathers.

If the whole Church is a family, with a father at every level of organization, it is easy to see how the literal family fits into that structure. God is our Father; the pope is our father; our bishop is our father; our pastor is our father; and within our homes, the Original Christians would have seen the literal father of the house as a kind of priest of a domestic church, the spiritual leader of that household. Another way to think about this is, if the Church is the Body of Christ, each of our homes is like one cell in that body. As such, the "nuclear family" is the basic building block of the household of the faithful. The head of the family home is the one responsible for leading and guiding the family members and for keeping them connected to the family of the Church.

One of the implications of this for the Original Church was that no one could be a "lone ranger" Christian. It is unfortunate that the agenda of the Protestant Reformation (to convince people to leave the Catholic Church for whichever particular brand of "reform" was being preached) ultimately redefined the concept of *conversion* in a way that has become a kind of "given" in Western Christianity—even among many Catholics. Conversion became the result of a process of logic, culminating in a decision. This makes it a very individualized commitment. But in the Original Church, conversion meant more than an intellectual change. It meant a complete change of lifestyle, from paganism, which had little to do with morality, to Christianity, with specific moral expectations for the baptized Christian. Furthermore, conversion was not seen as a moment in time but a process, or at least the beginning of a process, that was one with sanctification and would last the whole of one's lifetime.

The Protestant Reformation had to present conversion as a decision to be made and, once made, one that could be celebrated as an event that was done and, in a sense, completed. And so, conversion was redefined and came to be presented as something that happened in a Christian's past. At the same time, baptism—as the rite of initiation into the Church—also came to be redefined as a ritual commemoration of that decision made beforehand. In some cases, baptism was reduced to little more than an announcement to the community that a decision had been reached. But no early Christian would ever say, "I got saved on . . . " and recall a date in the past. They might refer to their baptism as the beginning of their faith journey (see 1 Pt 3:21), but conversion was always a process, never an event. Baptism was regenerative, at which time a person was "born from above" (not "born again"), but baptism was never thought of as the commemoration of a past event, such as a decision to commit one's life to Christ or a profession of faith. To be clear, the Original Christians did make decisions to commit their lives to Christ, but they knew that the regeneration of water and the Spirit took place in the sacramental moment of baptism itself, not at the moment they made the decision. They knew that baptism, as the initiation into the family of God, is a work of God, not primarily a human work. It is a sacrament, not the commemoration of a logical decision.

MYTH
Conversion and regeneration happen in a moment of decision. Baptism confirms and commemorates a decision already made.

TRUTH
Regeneration happens, and the process of conversion and sanctification begins, in the sacrament of baptism.

The point is that even conversion to Christianity is not really something that an individual does alone. Conversion is the submission of the self to something greater, which means becoming a part of a new family, but it also means giving up the "right" to be one's own highest authority and decide for oneself what is true and what is false. Conversion does not mean choosing which family to join based on the conclusions of your own logic; it means trusting the family that comes from Jesus and the apostles and entering into that family that has been a family since long before you arrived.

To refer to Jesus as one's "personal Savior" would have sounded strange to the Original Christians. Notice how virtually all of the prayers from the early Church are "we" prayers, not "I" prayers. They are meant to be prayed as part of the family, not so much as individuals. The Our Father is not the "My Father," and even when the early Christians prayed this at home and alone, they did not change it to "My Father." They said "Our Father" because they saw themselves as praying on behalf of their people.

Therefore, conversion is something done as part of a family, because through it one becomes a member of a new family, and because one cannot continue on the process of sanctification without the help of that family. In fact, it was common in the Original Church to welcome to membership whole families at a time—which means that the Original Church baptized whole families. It was never the case that the Church reserved baptism for adults only, as though one had to be a certain age to make the decision to commit to the Faith. This is because the Church recognized the reality of vicarious faith—for example, Jairus's daughter was healed on the basis of Jairus's faith (Mk 5: 21–43)—and the authority of the head of a household to make that commitment on behalf of his family and bring his whole family into the Church.

Even the original generation of Protestant Reformers did not dare to exclude infants and children from the grace of baptism. It was only in later waves of the Reformation that the individualism and emphasis on personal decision had taken such root that adult-only baptism was invented.

In the Protestant Reformation, the goal of preaching was to convince—through logic—one kind of Christian to become another kind of Christian. So the emphasis was on the intellectual, and therefore on the decision of an individual, rather than on the whole of life.

But in the Original Church, it was not so. Conversion was not simply a change of mind but a change of lifestyle, from non-Christian to Christian. Families often converted together, especially since they were going to have to live a new lifestyle together. And, on the basis of the faith of parents, and vouched for by sponsors, whole families were baptized.

On that first Pentecost, filled with the Holy Spirit, St. Peter preached the first Christian homily after the resurrection of our Lord. At the end of the homily, members of his audience asked him, "What should we do?" He answered, "Repent, and be baptized every one of you in the name of Jesus Christ so that your sins may be forgiven; and you will receive the gift of the Holy Spirit. For the promise is for you, for your children, and for all who are far away, everyone whom the Lord our God calls to him" (Acts 2:37–39). The Church Fathers knew that St. Peter's reference to children here was not meant to be interpreted as future generations, since Peter still thought Jesus would return within the lifetime of the apostles. And so, the Church baptized those whom the Lord called, as families, including children. Already in the Book of Acts, in chapter 16, we can see whole families getting baptized. The Church never restricted baptism according to age, and the only argument over the baptism of infants was whether or not to wait until the eighth day, in imitation of the Jewish rite of circumcision.

The only reason the New Testament does not include a lot of infant baptisms is because there was no second-generation Church yet, so infants and children were being baptized along with their parents, and in the Book of Acts especially, it simply wasn't the case yet that infants were being baptized at a later time than their parents. Later, in the fifth century, Pelagius argued that infants did not need baptism, and the Church declared that a heresy. The truth is, the Church Fathers affirmed the need for baptism of infants and children, on the basis of the fact that to deny it to them would be unmerciful (Mt 19:13–15). They are the most vulnerable members of the family, and they need the spiritual protection that comes with the grace of baptism, not to mention that this grace is what sets them on their life's journey of sanctification.

MYTH
One must be of an age of reason and make a personal decision for conversion in order to be baptized.

TRUTH
The Church has always baptized infants, children, and whole families.

On the other hand, the Original Church did not have a concept of "Once saved, always saved." Baptism regenerates, but it does not guarantee perseverance, let alone complete the process of sanctification. It begins the journey, but it was always assumed that even if one had accepted Christ as Savior, one could lose one's salvation if one rejected Christ through a lifestyle of habitual mortal sin.

It is ironic that some branches of Protestantism have created a theology of baptism that is the polar opposite of the Original Church's understanding. For the Original Church, baptism is regenerative but does not guarantee salvation. For many Protestants, baptismal regeneration is rejected, yet the baptism (or rather the decision to convert that it commemorates) guarantees salvation. In order to make this switch, and to do it without the sacrament of Confession, some Protestant groups had to create two new doctrines which were never believed in the Original Church. One is that all sin is equal in the eyes of God, and the other is that baptism washes away (or the faith decision results in forgiveness for) the sins one hasn't even committed yet.

MYTH
Baptism washes away all your sins, past, present, and future; therefore, you cannot lose your salvation.

TRUTH
Baptism washes away original sin, and all past sins, but future sins will require the sacraments for forgiveness. Without the sacraments, especially the Eucharist and Confession, you can fall from grace and lose salvation.

When Christians committed mortal sins after baptism, the early Church did not rebaptize them but rather developed and formalized the sacrament of Confession. There was a controversy over this in the early Church, and some did advocate rebaptism, but in the end, Pope St. Stephen clarified that only if a person had received a heretical baptism (that is, not a valid baptism in the name of the Father, Son, and Holy Spirit) would a person need baptism—but this would not be a rebaptism, since the previous heretical washing would not count as a baptism. Nevertheless, some Protestant groups today rebaptize those who have been validly baptized, because they misunderstand the criteria for a valid baptism (for example, they dismiss infant baptism, or they think that the way the water is applied matters), and some groups even rebaptize their own after supposed "backsliding." But the Original Church taught that baptism could not be repeated, as long as it was done with water and in the name of the Father, Son, and Holy Spirit. Rebaptism of someone validly baptized was considered an act of schism against the universal Church, as it still is.

MYTH

All sin is equal in the eyes of God, and you can just confess your sins to God in your heart.

TRUTH

Some sins are deadly, that is, "mortal" (1 Jn 5:16–17), and for these the Church offers the sacrament of Confession, penance, and reconciliation.

We Care for Their Bodies

Therefore, on behalf of those whom we call brothers or sisters, and other designations of relationship, we exercise the greatest care that their bodies should remain undefiled and uncorrupted.

–Athenagoras, *A Plea for the Christians*, 32

With regard to children, the Original Church, as a family, understood that they were to be protected, especially from predatory customs of the Romans, which by law gave older men the "right" to corrupt and abuse boys. The Church Father Clement of Alexandria, when mentioning the Ten Commandments, often included an eleventh, "Thou shalt not seduce boys." Women, too, and the marriage bed, were to be protected from exploitation. Finally, the early Christian prohibition of abortion, and the fact that it was considered to be a form of murder by the original Christians, is so widely attested that a whole book could be written on that subject. I'll have more to say about these topics in the following chapters.

So, what does it mean for us that the Original Church was a family? If we are to learn from the earliest Christians how to sanctify our everyday lives, we would train ourselves to think of the whole Church, and especially our parishes, as extensions of our own family. It's very easy to slip into a schedule that compartmentalizes the parish, separate from the rest of life and crammed into a small box on the calendar marked "Sunday." But to live like that is not to be part of a family.

It could be that those of us who are the "family-fathers" of our households have room for improvement in embracing our role in the sanctification of our families. Do we get our families to Mass, not just on Sundays, but on the holy days? Do we gather our families for prayer in the domestic church of our homes? Do we, as parents, both fathers and mothers, model a life of prayer and attention to spirituality? Do our kids see us going to Confession? Do they see us reading the Scriptures and/or the writings of the spiritual masters? Do they see us make of our lives a rhythm of work and devotion, feasting and fasting, not giving an unbalanced amount of time and attention to work outside the home? Do they see us give to our clergy the respect owed to fathers? Do they see us practice devotion to our Blessed Mother? Do they know that we financially support our parish and religious communities? Do they see us make it a priority to support the protection of the unborn, the vulnerable, the innocent, and to give special respect to the humble?

If you're thinking that you're too busy to add anything to your life right now, that is a valid concern. What that means, though, is that there may be things we need to remove from our lives to make room for the family of the Church and for the spiritual welfare of our households. If we have family members who are getting in the way of our sanctification and that of our family, do we prioritize the Church as our primary family? It may be that we need to decrease time spent with biological family members or in-laws who create obstacles to our sanctification, either by setting a bad example for our children or by getting us caught up in controversy and drama. And it may be that, if we work at a job that prevents the pursuit of holiness, we might need to find other work—and that, too, will come up in another chapter below.

Finally, be aware of the distinction between the non-sacramental theology that many Protestant denominations have with regard to not only matrimony, holy orders, and Confession, but even Holy Communion (which is often presented as merely a symbolic gesture, done—sometimes grudgingly—simply because Jesus told us to) and baptism (which is often presented as a rite of passage, commemorating a decision). And do not be taken in by Protestant arguments against infant baptism, or worse, allow yourself to be rebaptized. If you have been baptized in the Catholic Church—or any legitimate Christian communion for that matter—that is, if you have been baptized with water (regardless of the amount of water) and in the name of the Father, Son, and Holy Spirit, then you have been validly baptized and do not need rebaptism. Rebaptism is an offense against God, who was at work in the first baptism, against catholicity (we believe in one baptism), and even against ecumenism, since it usually disrespects another legitimate Christian church or communion. Therefore, it is an act of schism against the universal Body of Christ. The Original Church knew and taught that the sacraments are not simply rites of passage; they are not the work of humans, but they are the work of God in the moment, and the person who receives the sacrament is never the same, *because of* the sacrament. Ultimately the Church is sacramental because the Church is defined by the sacraments, as we are about to see.

MYTH

Ordination recognizes a person's sense of calling to ministry and the presence of God-given gifts and talents for ministry.

TRUTH

Holy orders may include the above, but it is primarily a sacrament in which the person being ordained receives from God the grace necessary for the vocation to which he is being ordained.

CHAPTER THREE

We Receive These Things

Among us, this food is called The Eucharist. Only those who believe that the things we teach are true, and who have been washed with the washing that is for the remission of sins and regeneration, and who are living as Christ has commanded are allowed to partake of it. For we receive these things, not as common bread and common drink, but just as the Word of God became flesh as Jesus Christ our Savior, and had both flesh and blood for our salvation, so we have been taught that in the same way, this food that would nourish our own flesh and blood by being metabolized but which is now blessed by the prayer of his word, is the flesh and blood of that Jesus who was made flesh.

–St. Justin Martyr, *First Apology*, 66

When we think about how the earliest Christians thought of themselves, and how they understood what the Church was, there are three aspects of this, all of which can be understood under the umbrella of "things received." And that makes sense, because early Christians would never have thought you could join something and then change it to suit your own desires. As we noted in the last chapter, to become a member of the

Church means to submit to something greater than yourself, and that means giving up the "right" to make yourself your own higher power by taking the authority to choose what you will accept as true and what you will reject as false.

The pagan world wants you to believe that there really is no absolute true and false, but only what you decide to be so, based on your own experience and preferences. But to be a Christian is to accept what is received from those who were Christians before you (even if you happened to be one of the early Christians and there were not as many who came before you). It means trusting the tradition and the process of handing it down, because at the end of the day, you cannot make up truth for yourself, you can only receive it. In fact, it is a principle of our faith that no one can have (let alone give) anything that they have not first received.

So, what are these "things received"? First of all, Christianity itself was defined by orthodox, or *correct*, doctrine. To be a Christian is to "believe that the things we teach are true," as St. Justin Martyr explained. Eventually the ecumenical councils of Nicaea (in AD 325), Constantinople (in AD 381), and Ephesus (in AD 431) would clarify the Church's defining doctrine of the Trinity, and the first two of those councils would produce the Nicene Creed, our common, and self-defining, statement of faith. Second, the early Christians were a Eucharistic people, who thought of themselves as those who gather around a table to receive the

Real Presence of Jesus Christ in the sacrament. And third, the early Christians saw themselves as part of something even greater than the whole Church on earth. The Church, to them, included all those who had gone before them and from whom they had received everything. In other words, the Church includes the saints in heaven. In this chapter, we'll look at each of these three aspects of Christian identity.

We Do Not Indulge in a Variety of Opinions

With us, there is no desire for vanity, and we do not indulge in a variety of opinions. For having renounced what is popular and earthly, and obeying the commandments of God, and following the law of the Father of immortality, we reject everything which rests on human opinion.

–Tatian, *Address to the Greeks*, 32

We have already noted how the Church was absolutely inclusive of all people, and this was no small matter in the context of Greco-Roman culture. But although the Original

Church welcomed all people, it did not welcome all ideas. To be accepting of all people meant welcoming them to "come as you are," but it did not mean allowing them to stay that way. And it certainly did not mean allowing them to bring in with them elements that were contrary to the teachings of Jesus and the apostles.

In fact, the earliest heresies in the Church were the result of converts trying to bring with them elements of the religions they had left. The so-called Judaizers, and their successors the Ebionites and other adoptionists, proposed a view of Jesus Christ that reduced him in their eyes to a prophet—someone who was anointed by God but was nevertheless a mere human. To these factions, Jesus was not the Son of God, if that implied a divine nature. And so, their heresy was to deny the divinity of Jesus. At the other extreme, the early docetics and then the gnostics tried to bring some of their polytheism with them. They had no trouble with the divinity of Christ (though they thought of him as *a* god, not *the* God). Their problem was with the Incarnation—that is, the idea that a divine being could also become human. So they denied the reality of Christ's humanity. But the apostles and their successors taught that Jesus Christ is *both* divine and human.

But really, what difference does it make? Didn't the Church accept all sincere ways of following Jesus? No, it didn't. Alternatives could not be tolerated, because to describe Christ incorrectly was to describe a *different*

Christ—one who does not exist and therefore one who cannot actually reconcile us to God. And so, throughout the early controversies over doctrine, the Church Fathers clarified the teachings of the Church and, in doing so, they clarified the very definition of what a Christian is—a Christian is one who believes what the Church teaches. No one gets to redefine Christianity according to alternative christologies (ways of understanding Christ); and no one gets to call himself a Christian and at the same time claim the permission (or the authority) to disbelieve or change the teachings of the Church. The Church was never a place where there were no wrong answers. There were wrong answers, and wrong answers do not lead to salvation.

Now, at this point I need to take a step back and clarify something. There is another myth about the early Church, mostly circulated by Protestant scholars, though sadly, some Catholic scholars have also jumped on this bandwagon. The myth is that there was no such thing as orthodoxy in the early centuries of the Church.

As the myth goes, the early Church was characterized by several (or many) competing—but equally valid—perspectives on Jesus Christ and the Trinity (some of them not Trinitarian at all), and what we now call orthodoxy is simply a label we stick on the winner of the debates. The implication is that any of them could have been the winner, but (here's where various myths about the invasive role of the emperor Constantine come in) politics took over, and Nicene Trinitarianism won the day. Therefore, the myth concludes, it is only after the ecumenical councils of the fourth century and the eventual acceptance of the Nicene Creed that we can talk about orthodoxy.

But all of that is false. The truth is that every generation of the early Church knew what orthodox doctrine was and what heresy was. The apostles knew what orthodoxy was, as opposed to the early docetics and the Judaizers. St. Ignatius of Antioch knew what orthodoxy was, as opposed to docetics and Ebionites. Sts. Justin Martyr, Clement of Alexandria, and Irenaeus of Lyons all knew what orthodoxy was, as opposed to gnosticism and adoptionism. Tertullian, Hippolytus, and Novatian all knew what orthodoxy was, as opposed to modalism and adoptionism. And so on. In every generation of the Church's life, there was a *mainstream* Church (the true Church), guided by the bishops as successors of the apostles. And the orthodoxy of the mainstream Catholic Church in any given generation is that which is most consistent with the orthodoxy of the previous generation.

There were also groups on the fringes of the Church presenting alternative explanations of the Person of Jesus Christ (christology) and his relationship to the God of the Old Testament. We call these alternatives *heresies*, a word that means a deviation from the straight and true. It's the doctrinal version of the biblical definition of sin—to miss the mark by straying to one side or the other. At the risk of oversimplification, the docetics, the gnostics, and (in a different way) the modalists strayed too far by emphasizing the divinity of Christ to the point where they denied his humanity; and the Ebionites and other adoptionists strayed too far toward the humanity of Jesus and denied his divinity. The mainstream Church—and there was always a mainstream Church—kept a middle path between these extremes. Rejecting the *either/or* answer to Jesus's question "Who do you say that I am?" they affirmed the *both/and*: Christ is both truly human and fully divine.

So, was the Original Church orthodox? Of course it was—because it was the Original Church (the Church Fathers) who defined what orthodoxy is. Was the Original Church Catholic? Of course it was, because the word *catholic* means *the whole Church*, and the whole Church was the mainstream Church. To be clear, to be on the fringes—to be outside the *mainstream* Church—was to be outside of the Universal Church. As St. Ignatius of Antioch wrote just before his martyrdom in about AD 110:

> Let no one do anything connected with the Church without the bishop. A valid Eucharist is one which is (presided over) by the bishop, or by (a priest) to whom he has delegated it. Wherever the bishop is, that is where the people should be, just as wherever

> Jesus Christ is, that is where the catholic Church is. (St. Ignatius of Antioch, *Letter to the Smyrnaeans*, 8)

In other words, the "catholic" Church—the whole Church, the true Church—is that assembly that gathers under the authority of the bishop who is in succession from the apostles.

Now, we need to be clear about what orthodoxy is and what it is not. It is not something that is completely static. To say that orthodoxy must be static would be to apply a kind of fundamentalism to Catholicism. The truth is that doctrine develops over time. This means that doctrine expands—it gets "fleshed out," so to speak. Doctrine gains in nuance and precision and comes to be further clarified and increasingly explained over time. On the other hand, doctrine does not "evolve," if by that one means a change from one thing into another. Therefore—and this is important—what is heresy in one generation can never become orthodoxy in a later generation. That would be a corruption, not a development. And what is orthodox in one generation cannot be declared heresy later—in fact, the orthodoxy of every generation becomes the foundation for the orthodoxy of later generations. Or to say it another way, the orthodoxy of any given era in the Church's history is built on the orthodoxy of previous eras. Therefore, we could define orthodoxy in any given generation as that which most faithfully receives and hands on the orthodoxy of the previous generations.

So, when we say that doctrine develops, we mean that it is clarified, but without being corrupted. Doctrine develops, but it does not "evolve." Tradition preserves that which is timeless, but it grows over time. It is not like keeping a petrified piece of wood on a shelf. It's more like tending to a living tree that grows, or perhaps like adding wood to a fire to keep a flame going. And so, the idea of a static Church without development is itself as much of a heresy as the idea of a Church that "evolves" by changing with the times. A Church without development would be as dead as a stone idol. But a Church that follows the winds of change would only be as alive as an amoeba: It has no backbone, and it would only keep splitting.

MYTH

There were many "christologies" in the early Church, all of them equally valid.

TRUTH

There was always a "mainstream" Church, the true Church, which is the Catholic Church, which received and handed on orthodox doctrine through the succession of bishops.

So, Tatian's statement above, that we do not indulge in a variety of opinions, means that the Original Christians saw themselves as people who received a tradition, and that tradition defined the very nature of the Church to which they belonged and the very nature of who they were as members of that Church. To deviate from the Tradition was to leave the Church. The Church itself was defined according to the doctrines received from those who came before, in an unbroken line going back to the apostles and to Jesus. We call this unbroken line *apostolic succession*.

What were the specific doctrines which the Original Christians understood to be the very definition of Christianity? The most important and defining doctrine of the Church is the doctrine of the Trinity, along with everything that goes with it, including the divinity of Jesus Christ, his virgin birth, his saving passion, his bodily resurrection, and the reliability of the Scriptures as God's revelation about all of it—in short, everything that's in the Nicene Creed. And that's no coincidence, since the Nicene Creed was specifically written to be the definition of orthodox Christianity, in opposition to heresy.

Therefore, the first answer to the question "What is a Christian?" is this: A Christian is Trinitarian. This means, of course, that those groups that are not Trinitarian cannot properly be called Christian. I don't mean Protestants—most of them are Trinitarian, and so as long as they accept the doctrines of the Nicene Creed, they are Christians—they are our brothers and sisters in Christ, though "separated brethren," divided from us. No, I mean groups such as

Jehovah's Witnesses and Unitarians. And that's not just me talking; that's the ecumenical councils of the Original Church.

I should point out, in case anyone might misunderstand, that we're not saying being a Christian requires perfect understanding of these doctrines. Everyone's understanding is imperfect to some extent, and even those who are intellectually challenged are not less in the kingdom of God. No, the requirement is not *understanding* so much as *acceptance* of the doctrines that we have received. To accept the teachings of the Church, even (or especially) when we doesn't understand them, is an act of faith and humility. To reject the defining doctrines of the Church, whether we understand them or not, is an act of pride, which of course is a mortal sin.

Some of the Church Fathers went so far as to say that heresy was necessary in order to push the Church to define what true belief and teaching should be. There's definitely some truth in that. But what is even more important for us to see, looking at the ecumenical councils in hindsight, is that the heretics were reading the same Scriptures as the mainstream Catholic bishops and theologians. Notice—the same Bible produced both orthodoxy and heresy! What that should tell us is that the meaning of Scripture is not plain and on the surface for all to see, as some would claim. The Scriptures need to be interpreted, and interpreting Scripture is not easy (all the Church Fathers would admit this). In fact, at the Council of Nicaea, it was the heretics, the Arians, who were arguing for a creed written from "Scripture alone." Yes, you read that right: the Arians were the *sola Scriptura* party in the time of the early Church.

But the orthodox bishops knew that the only way to interpret Scripture correctly is to use the Tradition of the Church to help you, much like lawyers use legal precedent, asking the question "How has this been interpreted by those who came before us?" In fact, the use of Tradition to interpret Scripture was itself an important part of the development of doctrine over time. Truth reinforced truth, as the boundaries of orthodoxy kept biblical interpretation from straying off into heresy, and ongoing biblical interpretation contributed to the development of the Church's clarifications of orthodoxy. As I always tell my students, all heresy is the result of trying to interpret Scripture apart from Tradition. We need what has been handed down to us to help us.

The Protestant doctrine of *sola Scriptura*, for many a defining doctrine of Protestant Christianity, usually assumes that somehow Scripture and Tradition are at odds. "Scripture alone" implies "Scripture without Tradition," and yet what that viewpoint fails to see is that Scripture *is* Tradition—it is simply that part of our Tradition that was written down by patriarchs, prophets, and apostles, and that we believe to have been inspired by God on a level that makes it infallible and authoritative for us. So, it is not the case that Scripture comes first and Tradition is some kind of addition to it, or worse, a deviation from the message of Scripture. The truth is that Tradition came first—even in the Church, when the apostles handed down Jesus's teachings, *and their interpretations of them*, before any of the New Testament was ever written down.

St. Paul tells us that he first confirmed his own beliefs with the apostles who knew Jesus, before he ever taught them to anyone else, and the very things he taught he describes with the same Greek word translated as "traditions." He says, "I commend you because you remember me in everything and maintain the traditions just as I handed them on to you" (1 Cor 11:2). So, Tradition is not opposed to Scripture. Scripture is, in fact, a part of the Tradition of the Church. Ironically, the doctrine of *sola Scriptura* is self-contradictory, since the Bible does not teach the doctrine of *sola Scriptura*. Nowhere in Scripture does the phrase "Scripture alone" appear, and nowhere does Scripture make this false dichotomy between Scripture and Tradition. To argue for a Church that follows Scripture, without Tradition and the development of doctrine, would be to argue for a Church that is not allowed to have church buildings, organs, or microphones, but one that would be allowed to have polygamy and slavery.

MYTH
The Protestant doctrine of *sola Scriptura* is patterned after early Christianity.

TRUTH
The Original Christians knew they needed Tradition to interpret Scripture.

This brings us back to the original myth of a supposed pre-Catholic Christianity. Were the Original Christians "Bible only" Christians? No, they were not. The Original Christians did not even have their own Bibles, and until the fourth century, there was no universal consensus on the table of contents of the Christian Bible. Another thing I always try to remind my students is that there is something in every Bible that is not Scripture. That is the table of contents. To speak of *Scripture alone* begs the question of what Scripture is, and it was the Original Church that defined which documents would be part of the Christian Bible—that is, which documents would be considered inspired enough to be universally authoritative. And in another great irony, the Original Church included those so-called deuterocanonical books of the Old Testament which Protestant Christianity has deleted from their Bibles. So, in spite of the claim that the Protestant Reformation was an attempt to get back to Original Christianity, the truth is that the Reformation moved farther from the Original

Church, by both stripping away legitimate developments and adding newly invented corruptions.

MYTH 1
The New Testament came before the Church, and the Church was patterned after the Bible.

MYTH 2
The Church did not have a Bible until the fourth century.

MYTH 3
The original Bible was the Protestant Bible, and Catholics added books to the Old Testament later.

TRUTH
The Christian Bible developed organically over the first four centuries of the Church; most of the New Testament was established by the early second century, but some of the other documents took longer to be confirmed. The Bible of the apostles and Church Fathers included all the books in the Catholic Bible. It was Protestants who took out some of the Old Testament books many centuries later.

Finally, it needs to be said that the early Christians' belief in the Trinity was not just something that lived in their heads. Christianity has always been an embodied faith, and Christians have always worshipped God with their whole bodies—standing, and kneeling, and anointing with oil, smelling incense, and consuming the elements of the Blessed Sacrament. And so, they also identified as Christians, and identified with the Blessed Trinity, by marking the Trinity on their bodies; that is, by making the Sign of the Cross. The myth that I was told, that Protestant expressions of Christianity are somehow more like the early Church, always implied that those things that we thought of as specifically Catholic were things that were added later, perhaps in the Middle Ages, and that were part of an overall departure from Original Christianity. And of course, we assumed that the making of the Sign of the Cross fell into this category.

But listen to what the Church Father Tertullian wrote around the turn of the third century:

> At every forward step and movement, and every going in and out, when we put on our clothes and shoes, when we bathe, when we sit at table, when we light the lamps, sit down on a couch or seat, in all the ordinary actions of daily life, we trace upon the forehead the Sign. (*On the Crown*, 3)

Although we do not see direct references to the making of the Sign of the Cross in the New Testament, the tradition began very early in the life of the Church, probably starting from the anointing associated with the sacraments. When someone was anointed, the bishop or priest made the Sign of the Cross on them with oil. Notice that in the Book of Revelation, to be baptized is described as being marked with the "seal." This is the anointing with oil, no doubt with the Sign of the Cross, and it is the opposite of the "mark of the beast" (Rv 7:3; 13:16–17). St. Cyprian would write, "In this Sign of the Cross is salvation for all who are marked on their foreheads" (*To Demetrianus*, 22).

This "sealing" with the Sign soon developed into the practice of making the Sign of the Cross at other times, even when there was no anointing, and you can see from Tertullian that the Original Christians made the Sign of the Cross often. Now, as a scholar, I have to admit that Tertullian may be exaggerating a bit. In other words, what we get in that quotation might be a little more of a wish list than what was actually happening. Maybe *some* people crossed themselves every time they put on their shoes or sat down on a chair, but maybe not everyone. Nevertheless, the point is that when Tertullian writes this, he expects that his audience knows what he's talking about and will accept it without serious contradiction—and that the Christians' non-Christian neighbors have seen them making the Sign of the Cross. We even have stories of martyrs, who were executed for their faith in times of persecution because they gave themselves away as Christians by making the Sign of the Cross in public.

And so, far from being a later add-on, Christians have always made the Sign of the Cross. And far from being a specifically Catholic thing, most Christians in the world, to this day, make the Sign of the Cross. The Original Christians saw the Sign of the Cross as a way of identifying themselves as Christians, and also as a blessing and as a prayer of protection. Several of the early Church Fathers commented on how the Sign of the Cross was a powerful prayer of protection against evil. St. Athanasius said, "By the Sign of the Cross, demons fly, oracles cease, all magic and witchcraft is brought to nothing" (*On the Incarnation*, 47–48). And the *Apostolic Tradition* said that the Sign of the Cross is a shield against evil, especially in times of temptation (*Apostolic Tradition*, 42). Incidentally, you can see from these quotations of the Church Fathers that the Original Christians made the Sign of the Cross on their foreheads, much like we still do at the reading of the Gospel. No one knows exactly when it got "bigger," covering the whole upper body, but it was probably the result of people mirroring the bishop's way of blessing a whole congregation.

MYTH

The cross was not used as a symbol for the Church until after Constantine.

TRUTH

Christians have always made the Sign of the Cross.

On the Day Called Sunday . . . We Gather

And we always keep together, and for everything we have been given, we thank the Maker of all through his Son Jesus Christ, and through the Holy Spirit. And on the day called Sunday, all who live in cities or in the country gather together in one place.

–St. Justin Martyr, *First Apology*, 67

This is how St. Justin Martyr begins his description of what the Original Christians were doing in their liturgies. It looks very much like our Mass, which is just one more piece of evidence that it is not in the Protestant expressions of Christianity that we will find the Original Church. If you were to go into a traditional Protestant church and look down the center aisle, what would you see? What is the focal point of the church's architecture? It's the pulpit. This is because for the Protestant, the sermon is the centerpiece of worship. The preaching of the gospel, often for "conversion," is the heart of worship. If a Protestant were to go to church on a Sunday, and there were no sermon, he might feel as if he didn't have church. But he can go to church week after week without receiving Communion and not worry about that.

Now think about a Catholic church. What is the focal point? It's the altar-table where the Sacrifice of the Eucharist takes place. A Catholic would not expect to have

Mass without the Sacrament. As St. Paul said, the *Eucharist* is actually the primary proclamation of the gospel: "For as often as you eat this bread and drink the cup, you proclaim the Lord's death until he comes" (1 Cor 11:26).

MYTH

The heart of Christian worship is the sermon; the focus is on the pulpit, and preaching is for conversion.

TRUTH

The heart of Christian worship is the Sacrifice of the Mass; the focus is on the altar-table, and preaching is for the interpretation of the Gospel and other Scriptures, for their application to daily life.

Just as the doctrine of "Scripture alone" is a corruption of Original Christianity, so is the Protestant doctrine of "salvation by faith alone" (*sola fide*). One could write a whole book about this and how Jesus himself never preached anything like "faith alone." In fact, the only place where the phrase "faith alone" appears in the Scriptures is where James says, "You see that a person is justified by works and *not* by faith alone" (Jas 2:24, emphasis added). All of the Church Fathers understood this and knew that one had to read Paul's contrast of faith versus the law (the law, not works) in light of Jesus's teachings and James's clarification. St. Justin Martyr would be just one example of this, when he wrote,

> And let those who are not found living as (Jesus) taught, be understood *not to be Christians*, even though they profess with their mouths the precepts of Christ. For it is not those who make a profession, but those who do the works, who will be saved, according to his word (when he said), "Not everyone who says to me Lord, Lord, shall enter into the Kingdom of Heaven, but the one who does the will of my Father who is in heaven." (*First Apology*, 16, emphasis added; see Mt 7:15–23)

In any case, it is enough for our purposes here to point out that there *are* some works which are *required* for salvation. These include forgiving others (Mt 18:23–35) and, especially for early Christian self-identity, regular reception of the Eucharist. Jesus said, "Remain in me, and I will remain in you. . . . Whoever does not remain in me is thrown into the fire"(paraphrasing Jn 15:1–6). And *how* do we remain in him? He answers that question in another place in John's Gospel. Jesus said,

> Very truly, I tell you, unless you eat the flesh of the Son of Man and drink his blood, you have no life in you. Those who eat my flesh and drink my blood have eternal life, and I will raise them up on the last day; for my flesh is true food and my blood is true drink. Those who eat my flesh and drink my blood remain in me, and I in them. Just as the living Father sent me, and I live because of the Father, so whoever eats me will live because of me. This is the bread that came down from heaven, not like that which your

> ancestors ate, and they died. But the one who eats this bread will live forever. (Jn 6:53–58)

How do we remain in him, and he in us? By coming, again and again, to his altar where his passion is re-presented, and his own flesh and blood are offered, and by turning that altar into a table where we take his flesh and blood into ourselves. But to neglect the regular reception of the Eucharist is just that kind of lifestyle of sin that could make one lose salvation.

Incidentally, the Original Christians did receive the Eucharist in the hand. They were very careful to protect it from desecration, and would be horrified to drop it on the ground, but self-contained hosts that could be popped into the mouths of the faithful by the presider were not invented until about the year 1000. St. Cyril of Jerusalem wrote that those receiving the Eucharist should place their hands in the form of a cross: "Make your left hand a throne for your right, as for that which is to receive a King. And having hollowed your palm, receive the Body of Christ, saying over it, Amen" (*Catechetical Lecture*, 23.21). Other early Christian documents which criticize certain behaviors do so on the assumption that what you do with your hands matters, since you will go to Mass and receive the Body of Christ in those same hands. Therefore, it is not necessary to worry about whether or not we should receive in the hand. The Original Christians did.

In the Original Church, too, the liturgy was celebrated in Greek until the third century, and then it changed to Latin, only in the West. The switch to Latin was a change to the vernacular, in the same way that the Second Vatican Council authorized liturgy in the vernacular languages. So, we should also not worry about whether one prefers Mass in Latin or English, since this was not a concern in the Original Church.

Remember that in the time of the Original Church, you could not walk down the street and see *a church*. The Church was not a building, and it wasn't even really a place, though I will talk about sacred space in the next section. For the early Christians, the Church was people, yes, but you can still talk about "going to church." So, what does it mean to "go to" church, if the Church is not a place? To go to church meant to go to the local gathering of the whole Church, and that gathering was around a table. Now, in the interest of full disclosure, the early Christians didn't really refer to it as a "table" that much, but I'm using that image to make us think of that aspect of the sacrament of the Eucharist that is a spiritual meal. If, as we have seen, the Church is a family, it is a family that gathers around a table. To be sure, the Church is made of the people who are baptized in the name of the Trinity, but baptism is the initiation. The goal of initiation, or what we call the source and summit, is the sacrament of the Eucharist. And so, it's appropriate to think of the Original Church as defining itself around this sacrament. In other words, in the minds of the early Christians, *the Church* is *the table*.

So, the second answer to the question "What is a Christian?" is this: A Christian is a person who gathers at the table of the Eucharist and receives the Body and Blood of Christ. And it is worth noting that although the doctrine of the Trinity was the source of much controversy and debate in the early Church (which facilitated the clarification of the doctrines), there was *no* controversy, and *no* debate, over Eucharistic theology in the early Church. It was a given for all of the Church Fathers that just as "the Word became flesh" in the Incarnation, so the elements of bread and wine become the Body and Blood of Christ in the Sacrament.

MYTH
Jesus is only symbolically or metaphorically present in Holy Communion.

TRUTH
The sacrament of the Eucharist offers us the Real Presence of Christ's Body and Blood.

In the Original Church, and consequently in Catholicism to this day, Christianity is an embodied faith. It is not something that is conceptual, or intellectual only. Our faith is lived in our bodies as we worship with our whole selves, and our bodies enact our faith in the world, primarily through works of mercy, as we will see in a later chapter. And this is because God has always chosen to mediate grace through the physical world of material things, not least of which is the Incarnation itself, when the Divine Word came into a human life.

The Protestant doctrine of "faith alone," on the other hand, had the effect (whether intentional or not) of making the Faith primarily intellectual, focused on a logical decision, based on the presentation of the gospel as information. This had the secondary effect of reducing the sacraments to rites of passage which commemorate human decisions but which were stripped of divine power in the moment of the sacrament itself. Eventually, in some branches of the Reformation, it also effectively individualized Christianity, as the conversion decision had to be made by an individual only (and an adult at that). All of this is ironically a version of the very gnosticism which the Original Church called out as heresy and opposed, and which minimized the works of mercy.

We Expect to Receive Again Our Own Bodies

Even after death, souls are in a state of consciousness . . . [and] we expect to receive again our own bodies, though they are dead and buried in the earth, for we maintain that with God, nothing is impossible.

–St. Justin Martyr, *First Apology*, 18

The Original Christians believed in resurrection. We know this from several Church Fathers, including St. Justin Martyr, who wrote whole treatises on the doctrine of the resurrection, aimed at rebutting contemporary philosophers who were scoffing at the idea. Some of those philosophers did believe in immortal souls, and a few of them believed in reincarnation, or the transmigration of souls into new bodies—but the idea that one could expect to get one's own body back? That was too much for them. This was because most of them couldn't bring themselves to believe that a physical body was worth redeeming. To these philosophers, and especially to the docetics and gnostics who took their philosophical dualism to the extreme, bodies were meant to be discarded.

The Christian belief in the resurrection is relevant here for two reasons. First of all, when Christians pass away and are gone from the present life, they have not left the Church. They are still an important part of the Body of Christ, which is—as we sometimes call it—a communion of saints. That communion exists across the divide between this life and the next, and the connection is not diminished by that divide. What the Original Christians believed was not simply that people "go to heaven" when they die, or even just that we will see them again in paradise. Those things are true, but it's more than that. The Original Christians believed that there is an unbreakable connection between a person's spirit and their body. Even though they may be separated for a time by physical death, that separation is only temporary. Salvation means that a person is redeemed whole, spirit and body, and that these are meant to be reunited. Of course, the body will be transformed, renewed, and made ready to be suited for a spiritual realm which is the heavenly kingdom of God (see St. Paul's thoughts on the resurrection body, or as he called it, the spiritual body, in 1 Cor 15). But it will be the same body we had in life, in much the same way as the butterfly is the same creature as the caterpillar, and yet the butterfly's transformed body is made, not for crawling, but for flight.

The second reason that resurrection is relevant for the early Christians' self-identity is that it gives all of life a certain long-term perspective that encourages the Christian to prioritize the things of eternity over the things of the present life. And the Original Christians lived and practiced this perspective by (among other things) visiting the tombs of those who had gone before them, praying at the tombs, and asking for those saints in paradise to intercede for them. The Protestant myth of the Original Church being like the "Reformed" denominations would have you believe that prayer for the intercession of the saints was something that came along later, a superstitious concession for people who missed worshipping many gods. But the actual evidence from early Christianity shows us that this is not true at all. The truth is that the Original Christians spoke to the saints in their prayers, asked them for their intercession, and when they could, they did so at their tombs. This is because of that unbreakable connection between the souls of the saints in heaven and their relics here on earth. The presence of the bodily remains of a Christian makes that place holy ground.

In the account of the martyrdom of St. Polycarp of Smyrna, we read about what the faithful Christians did with the body of their bishop:

> We took up his bones, as being more precious than the most exquisite jewels, and more proven than gold, and deposited them in an appropriate place, where, when the opportunity allowed us to gather together, the Lord would grant us to celebrate the anniversary of his martyrdom, with joy and rejoicing, in memory of those who have already finished their struggle, and for the training and preparation of those yet to walk in their footsteps. (*Martyrdom of Polycarp*, 18)

There are still examples of ancient graffiti from the early Christians at the catacombs, inscriptions scrawled on the walls near the tombs of the martyrs, asking for their intercession.

MYTH

Prayer for the intercession of the saints was a holdover from paganism and therefore is a form of idolatry.

TRUTH

Prayer for the intercession of the saints has always been a part of Christian spirituality and is grounded in the doctrine of the resurrection.

It is not true that the early Christians hid from the Romans in the catacombs. The catacombs were legally registered burial grounds, and so the Romans knew exactly where they were. Sometimes the early Christians did make secret back entryways into the catacombs, so the Romans wouldn't see them coming and going, but the catacombs were not protection from persecution. It is also not true that the early Christians held regular Masses in the catacombs, but they did worship there. In addition to funeral Masses, the Original Christians continued a Roman tradition called the *refrigerium*. This was a memorial meal, usually on the anniversary of a loved one's death. It was a kind of a picnic and, in the Roman mind, it was a way to share a meal with the one who had passed on. For the Original Christians, however, it was much more than that. It was a way to be in the very presence of a living saint, whose spirit was with Christ in paradise but whose body was close by. And to be close to the bodily remains was to be close to the person, who was close to God.

So the early Christians didn't just have a picnic; they worshipped at the tombs because they were on holy ground. They read the Scriptures and the stories of the saints' martyrdoms, they sang psalms and hymns, and they prayed for the souls in purgatory and for the saints' intercession. And when a bishop or priest was available, they had Mass, including Mass intentions for the departed. As the Church order manual known as the *Apostolic Didascalia* advised,

> Come together, even in the cemeteries, and read the Holy Scriptures, and without demur perform your ministry and your supplication to God, and offer an acceptable Eucharist, the image of the royal Body of Christ, both in your congregations and in your cemeteries, and on the departures of those who sleep . . . without doubting pray and offer for those who have fallen asleep. For those who have believed in God, even though they should sleep, they are not dead. (*Didascalia Apostolorum*, 26.22)

In the catacombs of Rome, often the lid of the sarcophagus was the altar of the Eucharist. And when it eventually came time to build the first Christian basilicas, they were built over the tombs, or the tombs were brought to them, and the very intimate connection between the bodies of the martyrs and the Body and Blood of the Lord in the Eucharist was built into the very architecture of the churches.

St. Ignatius of Antioch made this connection between death and the Eucharist when he wrote to the Christians at Rome. He was on his way to Rome, to be thrown to the lions in the Colosseum, and he said this of his impending martyrdom, requesting that the Roman Christians not try to rescue him:

> Allow me to be food for the wild beasts, through which I will go to God. I am the wheat of God, and I will be ground by the teeth of the wild beasts, so that I may become the pure bread of God. (St. Ignatius of Antioch, *Letter to the Romans*, 4.1)

And so, our third answer to the question "What is a Christian?" is this: A Christian is a person who sees the big picture of eternity, and lives life with a certain focus on the kingdom—seeking first the kingdom of God, you might say. We believe in an afterlife, of course, but more than that, we believe in the resurrection. This gave the Original Christians a unique attitude toward death, combining a Jewish respect for the body (though without considering it unclean) with a Roman respect for ancestors (but without cremating their bodies). Care for the bodies of the dead is a Christian work of mercy, after all (note the reference to "your ministry" in the quote from the *Didascalia*, above). The Original Christians prepared the bodies of their loved ones, not just for burial, but for resurrection. They believed that the remains of these bodies made a place holy, and they visited these holy places and worshipped God there. And they believed that a person's body was an essential part of their identity, not to be discarded, as the gnostics taught, or traded in for another one, as some of the philosophers taught. A soul cannot be put into another body, and a person cannot change who they are by changing their bodies. The resurrection is not receiving a different body, but receiving your own body back again, redeemed, renewed, and transformed for eternal life.

Putting all of this together, we can see that the Original Christians thought of themselves as existing in a succession of believers, receiving from those who came before, and passing on what was received to those who came after. As Christians, we do not exist in our own time only, but we are in a stream, so to speak, the recipients of a faith handed down to us by that great cloud of witnesses who came before us, and we are responsible for handing it on to our children and all those who come after us. And what have we received, and what have we been entrusted with handing on? We have received the definitive doctrine of the Trinity and all that goes with it, to help us at least begin to understand the God who is our Creator, and his son Jesus Christ. We have received the Body and Blood of Christ our Savior in the sacrament of the Eucharist, which is an essential part of receiving eternal life. And in the resurrection, we will receive again our bodies, redeemed for a wholeness we have never completely known in this life.

And so, what does it mean for us, today, that the Original Christian was a person who lived in a stream, flowing from those who came before, down to those who came after? If we are to learn from the earliest Christians how to sanctify our everyday lives, we would first and foremost make sure that our children understand that they, too, are in the stream, and they live as part of something greater than themselves. We should do our best to understand the core doctrines that define us as Christians, and how that makes us different from others who do not share those beliefs. We would, at the very least, put in the effort to understand the Nicene Creed, even if only at a beginner level, so that when we say it in Mass, we are truly professing our faith, and not just going through the motions of a rote "pledge of allegiance." We would also teach our children the value and miraculous nature of the Eucharist and foster an attitude in which one should be loath to miss any opportunity to receive the real Body and Blood. But we would not look down on or criticize those who receive the Sacrament in the hand or prefer Mass in English, because the Original Christians received the Eucharist in the hand and their Mass was in Greek.

We would identify with Christ, and identify ourselves as Christians, by making the Sign of the Cross often. And we would demonstrate our faith in the resurrection by taking care of the bodies of our loved ones, preparing them not just for burial but for resurrection. We would have our loved ones' funerals in churches, not funeral homes. It is true that it is now acceptable to cremate, but it is not acceptable to spread ashes, especially in places that do not maintain a reverence appropriate for holy ground.

CHAPTER FOUR

We Share Our Food, but Not Our Wives

For the Christians are not distinct from other people according to country, or language, or the customs they observe. They do not live in cities of their own, or speak with any particular dialect. . . . Rather, they live in Greek as well as barbarian cities, according to where their lot in life has determined, and by following the customs of their native land with respect to clothing, food, and the rest of their ordinary behavior, they show us their wonderful and admittedly paradoxical way of life. They dwell in their own countries, but simply as sojourners. As citizens, they share in all things with others, and yet endure all things as foreigners. . . . They marry, as everyone does, and they bear children, but they do not discard their unborn. They have a common table, but not a common bed. . . . To sum it all up in a word, what the soul is in the body, that is what the Christians are in the world. The soul is dispersed through all the members of the body, ,and Christians are scattered through all the cities of the world.

–"Mathetes," *Epistle to Diognetus*, 5–6

When it came to the catechesis of the Original Church, to prepare people for baptism, it was more important that they learn how to *live* as Christians than that they learn what to believe. Of course, they were taught the defining doctrine of the Trinity, on some level, and usually in the form of a creed. But for the most part, the bishops of the early Church assumed that it was only *after* baptism that people would have the grace to begin to understand the teachings of the Church and the meaning of the sacraments. With the possible exception of the philosophers who became the early apologists, most people did not choose to become Christian because they understood the doctrines. They chose to become Christian because they were putting their faith in the family they were joining.

MYTH

To become Christian, one listens to preaching until one understands the teachings enough to judge that they are true, and then one gets baptized as a way to acknowledge to the Church that one approves of the Church's doctrines (understanding leads to faith).

TRUTH

Becoming Christian means one has found the family of the Church to be both life-giving and trustworthy. One gets baptized to submit oneself to the Church, and then the grace of baptism facilitates the increasing understanding of the Church's teachings (faith leads to understanding).

Eventually, a post-baptismal catechesis called *mystagogia* developed, but the point here is that for most people who converted to Christianity from Greco-Roman culture, baptism would mean a radical change in *lifestyle*, and the bishops did not want to baptize anyone who did not go into it with eyes wide open to the reality of what was going to be expected of them in terms of morality. The vast majority of Greco-Roman religions were somewhere on a scale between patriotic civic clubs and fraternal lodges, without any real expectations about the moral conduct of their members. They had their ethics, but these tended to be utilitarian, and the overall rule was that if you could get away with something without causing you or your family dishonor, then the gods didn't really care what you did behind closed doors or how you treated other people. But this Christian God does care, and he sees everything, so there are no doors that are closed to God. The very idea of a religion in which a person was accountable to God for their everyday behavior would be a new thing for many people coming into the Church. To put it in terms we would use today, a newly baptized Christian was going to have a new relationship with the society and culture in which he or she lived. And that new relationship was going to have to be *countercultural*.

This statement that "We share our food but not our wives" (or as translated here, we "have a common table, but not a common bed") pops up in several of the works of the early apologists. The implication in all of these documents is that the very identity of a Christian—who we are—is defined by *what we don't do*. In the subtext of the documents, that means *the things that you Romans do, that we do not do*. That is what sets a Christian apart. Not nationality, or ethnicity, or language, or local customs (because all people are welcome), but morality.

The most obvious moral difference was that Christians did not worship the idols of the Greco-Roman gods, but this was just one of the sins a person might "backslide" into after baptism which would threaten his salvation. As I noted above, the Original Christians knew that all sins were not equal in the eyes of God, and that there were certain sins which were "unto death" (1 Jn 5:16). The general consensus seems to be that the three worst mortal sins a Christian could commit were idolatry, murder, and adultery—though not always in that order. Sometimes the Church Fathers speak of adultery as though it is the worst sin, but that's probably because it's the one that the early bishops were most concerned about. As we will see below, a lot of things we would consider to be forms of adultery were perfectly acceptable in Roman culture. The bottom line is that anyone converting to Christianity from paganism (and especially any *man*, and especially any *wealthy* man) would have to learn that a lot of behavior that he always considered his "right" was now going to be unacceptable. And he had to learn all this *before* his baptism, because you don't want to commit mortal sin after baptism. The Church took post-baptismal mortal sin very seriously, and this is part of the reason why we have a sacrament of Confession.

We Choose Life

There are two ways: one of life, and one of death, and a great difference exists between these two ways. The way of life, then, is this: First, you must love God, who made you; second, love your neighbor as yourself . . . you must not commit murder; you must not commit adultery; you must not corrupt boys . . . you must not practice magic; you must not practice witchcraft; you must not murder a child by abortion or by killing a newborn.

–*The Didache*, 1–2

The concept of the "two ways" comes from the Old Testament and is a common theme in Jewish and early Christian literature. In Deuteronomy chapter 30, we read the following:

> See, I have set before you today life and prosperity, death and adversity. If you obey the

> commandments of the LORD your God that I am commanding you today, by loving the LORD your God, walking in his ways, and observing his commandments, decrees, and ordinances, then you shall live and become numerous, and the LORD your God will bless you in the land that you are entering to possess. But if your heart turns away and you do not hear, but are led astray to bow down to other gods and serve them, I declare to you today that you shall perish; you shall not live long in the land that you are crossing the Jordan to enter and possess. I call heaven and earth to witness against you today that I have set before you life and death, blessings and curses. Choose life so that you and your descendants may live, loving the LORD your God, obeying him, and holding fast to him; for that means life to you and length of days, so that you may live in the land that the LORD swore to give to your ancestors, to Abraham, to Isaac, and to Jacob. (Dt 30:15–20)

And so, there are two ways, the way of life and the way of death. To follow in the way of God is to choose the way of life. Early Christian documents are also referring to this same concept when they warn people against being "double-minded" (for example, see Jas 1:8). To be double-minded is to profess belief in God, but not "walk the talk." It is to put your hand to the plow, but look back (Lk 9:62).

When it comes to practicing what we preach, the early Christians began with the Ten Commandments, as we would expect. Then, as you can see from the quotation of the *Didache* above, special emphasis was always placed on an adamant rejection of abortion and the exposure of babies. To the early Christians, both were forms of murder, and it didn't matter whether a baby was murdered before it was born or after, it was still murder. Ironically, Roman law didn't much care about whether the baby was preborn or newly born either. Killing a baby in either scenario was the right of the father, and many babies were killed—some before birth, with the use of drugs—but most after birth, by being drowned in a bucket. Those not killed were left on the garbage pile to die of exposure, to be killed by hungry wild animals, or to be picked up by pimps and raised to a life of slavery and prostitution.

So, who are the Christians? The Christians are those who do not kill their babies. In fact, the Christians are the ones you might see rescuing abandoned babies from the garbage piles. They considered these children orphans who needed to be rescued (Aristides, *Apology*, 15). In fact, virtually every apologetic document from the early Church makes the opposition to abortion and to the exposure of infants a hallmark of Christian identity. Minucius Felix wrote to a pagan Roman,

> I see that you, at one time expose your begotten children to wild beasts and birds, and at another time you kill them with a miserable kind of death by strangulation. And there are some women who drink drugs and potions, and by doing so, extinguish

> the source of the future man within them, and thus commit murder even before they deliver. . . . But to us it is not lawful to even see or hear of murder. (*Octavius*, 30; see also St. Justin Martyr, *First Apology*, 27–29)

Both St. Justin Martyr and Minucius Felix go on to say that when Romans expose their children, who are then raised to be prostitutes, it is only a matter of time before these same Romans, when visiting the brothels, will unknowingly commit incest.

We Protect Children from Corruption

And the way of death is this: First of all it is evil and full of curse—murders, adulteries . . . murderers of children, corrupters of the handiwork of God.

–*Didache*, 5

You may have noticed in the earlier quote from the *Didache* above, the phrase "You must not corrupt boys." It was common among upper-class Roman men—it was considered normal, even expected—for an older man to take on a boy and enter into a sexual relationship. It was considered a form of mentoring but was in fact pedophilia. The older man was thought to be guiding the boy into manhood, and as part of the Roman patron-client system, the man would continue on as the boy's patron, and the boy would become the man's client when he himself became a man. Other versions of this predatory system included "tutors" who were actually hired by parents to have this kind of relationship with their sons. One famous Roman poet even wrote a document giving advice on how to seduce young boys. All of this was based on the notion that before a boy's beard began to grow, he was not yet really a man, in the sense that we might say a male, and when the beard started to grow the boy could then choose whether to be a man (sexually dominant) or to continue on in the sexually submissive role. The fact is, many of these boys were not only corrupted, they were ruined, as they often did not really have the choices they were once promised, or if they did, they were too confused to make the right choice. Many of the early Christian apologists mention the case of Antinous, the teenaged boy who was in a relationship with the emperor Hadrian. Antinous drowned, probably a suicide. Hadrian then proclaimed him a god and put up statues of him all over the empire, which the early Christians saw as tragic monuments to Roman deviance.

In the quotation immediately above, the author(s) of the *Didache* actually give a long list of behaviors that characterize the way of death. Among these are the murder of children (by abortion or exposure) and the "corruption of God's handiwork." The Greek word for "handiwork" is one that is used for God's Creation of humans. I take this to be a reference to the sexual exploitation and corruption of children by Roman custom. In other words, the way of death is characterized not only by abortion and infanticide, but also by the predatory corruption of these "little ones" who are made in the image of God (Lk 17:2). Let us remember the "eleventh Commandment" of Clement of Alexandria: "Thou shalt not seduce boys." I've already noted that Christians protected the dignity and safety of innocent life. The point here is to emphasize that the original Christians saw themselves as living in a world which was *a threat to their children*. They saw themselves as people who need to protect their children from the culture around them.

We Do Not Practice Sorcery

My child, do not look for omens, since this leads to idolatry. Do not practice magic, or astrology, or incantations. You should not even want to look at these things, for they all lead to idolatry.

–*Didache*, 3

You may also have noticed, in that first quote from the *Didache*, the phrase "You must not practice magic; you must not practice witchcraft." Most of the documents also mention this as an identifying mark of a Christian. We might think this is obvious, and perhaps even less relevant in our own time, but that's only because sorcery can take different, more subtle, forms now. In the Roman Empire of the Original Church, an average day of running errands could include a visit to the oracle, where one might buy a peek into one's future, or a trip to the spell dealer, where one might buy a curse against one's neighbor. It should go without saying that these kinds of seeking after power are contrary to a life in relationship with God, but again, the point is that the original Christians lived in a world in which there was always an undercurrent of the buying and selling of spiritual power and information. In fact, we have documents that include the Roman equivalent of a prenuptial agreement, in which a wife promised not to cast any spells against her new husband. And this brings us to the early Christian commitment to matrimony.

We Do Not Share Our Wives

And so I will go on at once to exhibit the peculiarities of Christian society. . . . We do not hesitate to share our earthly goods with one another. All things are in common among us but our wives.

–Tertullian, *Apology*, 39

Echoing the *Epistle to Diognetus*, Tertullian explains what is different about Christians by giving a long list of the things we don't do. On that list, once again, we find the statement that we do not swap spouses. Why do the early apologists feel the need to mention this? Because this is one of the things that stood out to the average Roman as peculiar. Christians have very different ideas about marriage.

To begin with, marriage under Roman law was a business contract, made for the purpose of the consolidation and protection of wealth. A legally registered marriage was one in which two families had merged, like businesses, and in part, the contract was meant to prevent the "wrong" people from inheriting any of the wealth. In other words, it was simply assumed that a husband would have illegitimate children, but more important to the husband was the possibility that any child his wife bore might not be his (one reason why it was his legal right to kill it). All of this has the effect of turning marriage into something very different from the way Jesus talks about marriage in the Gospels. For one thing, divorce was easy and common. No reason was needed other than desire. In fact, a woman's father could initiate her divorce simply because he had found her a new match that would be better for the family business.

But what this also means is that for the vast majority of people, who were not wealthy, it was often the case that a legally registered marriage was unnecessary. For many Christians, a legal marriage may not even have been an option, since marriage across certain social class lines was illegal. For example, someone from the senatorial class could not legally marry a freedperson (former slave). Since the Church welcomed people from all classes as equals, and since wealthy men converted in lower numbers than anyone else due to the moral expectations and radical change of lifestyle, it was not uncommon for Christian women from the aristocratic classes to come together with men from the lower classes and to receive their bishop's blessing to be husband and wife and make a family, even though they could not be legally married.

This is not to claim that no one married for love in the Roman world. But most people did not bother with a legal marriage—and this includes the early Christians. The problem is that we don't know for sure which marriages were registered according to Roman law and which were not, since the Latin sources refer to all cohabiting couples as *husbands* and *wives*, whether or not they had the marriage contract. Most people, as far as we can tell, simply made a decision together to form a family. But of course, that added a layer of uncertainty about the family in question, which meant that the rug could be pulled out from under them at any time, and any women who did not come from wealthy families were especially vulnerable to destitution.

Holy matrimony is, at the same time, the first sacrament of them all, instituted by God in Genesis and endorsed by Jesus in the Gospels, and also the last of the sacraments to be fully formalized. In the first three centuries of the life of the Church, before the legalization of Christianity, all we know for sure is that there seems to be an expectation that Christian couples who wished to make a family should get the blessing of their bishop (mentioned in Ignatius of Antioch, *Letter to Polycarp*, 5). Whether there was a ritual for this blessing is uncertain; we have no evidence of it. In the absence of evidence, I think that there probably was some kind of marriage blessing ritual that developed relatively early, which may have coexisted alongside a parallel ritual for the consecration of religious celibates. It seems unlikely that the consecrated virgins would have a ceremony for becoming brides of Christ without those making the commitment to the vocation of matrimony having a ceremony too.

In any case, it was not until Christianity was legalized, and the emperor Constantine granted to Christian bishops the powers of civil magistrates (to do things like sign off on a marriage contract), that the Church was in a position to begin to standardize a ritual for the sacrament of matrimony. This is why clergy today are able not only to perform a wedding but also sign the government marriage license—but this is also why we have such confusion in our culture, which blurs the distinction between civil marriage and the sacrament of holy matrimony. Even by the time of St. Augustine, bishops complained that Christian couples were still incorporating too many of the old pagan practices into their weddings (some of which we still see today).

Therefore, the Original Church had the task of redefining marriage for anyone who came into the Church with the assumptions of Greco-Roman culture. Roman marriage was a business deal, complete with a deposit held in escrow (the dowry), which assumed that the head of the household was basically the owner of the family, and (in legal terms at least) his wife and children were his property. Even when the Romans did give more ownership rights to women, such as the right to inherit and will their property, it was still the case that a woman who gave birth to a girl might have no power to prevent her husband from killing her daughter. Christian matrimony, on the other hand, is a covenant of mutual servanthood. It is meant for the mutual sanctification of the couple and for the protection of the more vulnerable members of the family. And as we know from Scripture, Christian marriage is an image and revelation of God's love for humanity and Christ's love for the Church (see Eph 5).

As I hinted above, the Original Church also had to redefine adultery for those who came in from paganism. It was not enough to say that Christians don't commit adultery. The Romans might say the same thing, except that their definition of adultery was very narrow. Since marriage was a property contract, adultery under Roman law meant that one man was stealing another man's property (his wife). But a married man cheating on his wife with an unmarried woman, or a married man visiting the prostitutes, or having sex with a slave, none of this counted as adultery to the Romans. For the Romans, adultery was an offense against a man. For the Christians, adultery is an offense against God.

So, who are the Christians? The Christians are those who don't treat their spouses and children as property, to be exploited, abused, disrespected, or discarded. What this means for us in our contemporary context is that we can relate to the early Christians in some significant ways. We, too, live in a world that presents certain and serious dangers to our children. We, too, live in a world that defines both marriage and adultery differently than we do. As with the Original Church, what makes us different from the world around us is our morality. And we can see that in the early documents of the Church, the very identity of a Christian was often defined in terms of "what we don't do." The controversy around abortion in our culture demonstrates that this issue is just as much an indicator of countercultural Christianity as it has always been. A Christian is one who chooses life—who goes the way of life, not the way of death—and who is always open to life. A Christian is also one who "rescues the orphan," meaning that he supports the adoption of those children who might otherwise be discarded.

In recent years, another threat to children has emerged. Shockingly, we find that behavior once universally rejected is now open for discussion and is being championed by those unashamed of its corruption. We even find that the medical and psychological professions have been hijacked and made to subvert their oath to "do no harm." And so, like the Original Christians, we find that we have to be vigilant to protect our children from things our parents didn't need to worry about. This means that now more than ever in recent memory, parents are being called not only to be the models of the relationship between Christ and his Church, but also to be the protectors and defenders of marriage itself, and their children, and the family. To that end, it is important for us as Catholic Christians to maintain and clarify the distinction between civil marriage and the sacrament of holy matrimony.

When it comes to the family and the household, it cannot be overemphasized that we are also being called, in a way like never before in our lifetimes, to defend against the introduction of demonic forces through the practice of the occult. We live in a culture that sees horoscopes, tarot cards, psychics, and the like as harmless entertainment. But to engage in any of these things is to "practice sorcery." And as the *Didache* reminds us, this kind of seeking after power, or even information, only leads to idolatry, because it places something else in our lives as a rival to God for our trust. And what is more immediately dangerous, these practices and their related paraphernalia are quite literally invitations to the demonic to enter our homes.

CHAPTER FIVE

We Work for Your Benefit

We sojourn with you in the world—we do not avoid the forum, or the butcher shop, or the baths, or the stores, or the workshops, or the inn, or the weekly market, or any other places of commerce. We sail with you, and fight by your side, and till the ground with you, and in like manner we unite with you in your dealings. Even in the various arts, we make our work available for your benefit. How it is that we seem useless in your ordinary business, living with you and by you as we do, I am not able to understand.

–Tertullian, *Apology*, 42

In writing this, Tertullian's point was to emphasize how in almost every way, the Christian is not different from everyone around him. Of course, he would eventually get around to talking about how Christians *are* different, but here he points out that Christians work, shop, travel, participate in government, and even fight in the legions, alongside non-Christians. Christians do not keep to themselves or deal only with other Christians. In fact, as he says a few chapters earlier in the same document, "We are everywhere—the only place left where you won't find us is in the temples of your gods"(literally, "We have left nothing to you but the temples of your gods," *Apology*, 37). In other words, Christian work does not benefit only the individual worker and his family, or even only those within the Church. Christian work benefits everyone, because *we work so that we can share.*

We Show a Special Respect to the Lowly

Our feast explains itself by its name. In Greek it is called agape, that is, love. Whatever it costs, our outlay in the name of piety is gain, since with the good things of the feast we benefit the needy; . . . as it is with God himself, a special respect is shown to the lowly.

–Tertullian, *Apology*, 39

Probably more than a century before Tertullian wrote this, the Eucharist described by St. Paul in 1 Corinthians 11 had been moved out of the evening meal and had become a morning liturgy featuring the Sacrament—what we call the Mass. But the evening meal, the *agape*, or love-feast, continued on in the Church, as Tertullian describes, and it became a way for the early Christians to share their resources with those who were in need. The meal became, in effect, a kind of combination of a potluck dinner and a soup kitchen. The Church order document known as the *Apostolic Tradition* (its original core may have been written in the third century by Hippolytus) even says that after the agape meal, the leftovers should be sent out to those in need who could not be there (*Apostolic Tradition*, 28).

Toward the end of the second century, Clement of Alexandria wrote a treatise called *Who Is the Rich Man That Shall Be Saved?* The question comes from Jesus's statement that it is easier for a camel to pass through the eye of a needle than for a rich man to enter the kingdom (Mt 19:23–26; Mk 10:23–27; Lk 18:24–27). Having heard Jesus make this statement, the disciples responded by asking, "Then who can be saved?" Clement's answer is that it is not wealth, per se, that is a sin. It is the hoarding of resources—the refusal to share with those who have less—that gets in the way of a person's salvation. And here he speaks for the consensus of the Church Fathers. Most Christians need not renounce all money and possessions (though some are called to do that). Rather, most Christians are meant to live with the understanding that if God has given you resources, they are given to you specifically for the purpose of sharing them with others. As Clement says it:

> For the one who holds possessions, and gold, and silver, and houses, as the gifts of God, and ministers from them to the God who gives them for the salvation of others, and knows that he possesses them more for the sake of the brotherhood than his own, and is above being possessed by them, and so is not the slave of the things he owns, and does not carry them about in his soul, and does not let his life become bound or controlled by them, but is always laboring at some good and divine work, and even if at some time he should be compelled to be deprived of his possessions, he is able to bear their loss with a cheerful mind just as much as when he had plenty—this person is the one who is blessed by the Lord, and called poor in spirit, a fitting heir of the Kingdom of Heaven, not the one who was prevented from living with wealth. (*Who Is the Rich Man That Shall be Saved?*, 16)

To paraphrase what Clement is saying in more modern terms, Christians work so that they can "pay it forward," giving back to God by giving to others. As St. Basil said of his monks, "They work with their own hands, so that they may have something to distribute to those in need" (*Letter*, 207.2). In other words, if you have anything, then God has given it to you, and if God has given you anything more than what you need, that means God has given you a ministry. That ministry is to use your resources, as Clement said, "for the salvation of others." Incidentally, this should serve as a critique of those charities or ministries that feel it necessary to separate the help of those outside the Church from sharing the gospel with them. The Original Christians would hear Jesus's words to "let your light shine" as instruction to make sure people know *why* you do the good works you do, "so that they may see your good works and give glory to your Father in heaven" (Mt 5:16).

MYTH

It is unethical or somehow manipulative to share the gospel and invite into the family of the Church those to whom we minister with the works of mercy.

TRUTH

Although we would never require conversion or any commitment in order to help people, to help them without letting them know why we do what we do, and without offering an invitation to God's family, is to hide our light under a bushel.

In the Roman world, where manual labor was looked down upon and avoided, and not having to work was considered a right of noble birth (and perhaps that describes every time and place), the Church affirmed the dignity, and even sanctity, of work. Work itself sanctifies, and so it is not to be avoided. In fact, to avoid work is to be a burden on the community (2 Thes 3:7–12). However, it has to be made clear that the Original Church was not a commune, much less communistic. This may seem obvious to many of us, but I have heard people say that the early Church was communist, or more often simply operate on the assumption that the early Church was somehow Marxist. It was not, and the ways in which Marxism is incompatible with the Christian faith are too numerous to get into here. It is true that we do have this image of the early Church in Acts, chapter 2, that the original Christians "were together and had all things in common" (Acts 2:44). But notice the text does not say they *lived* together, and although they do seem to have pooled their money, this was entirely voluntary. (Ananias and Sapphira met their end not because they held money back, but because they lied to the apostles.) In any case, this arrangement didn't even last to the end of the Book of Acts, mostly because—as I noted above— the gospel had to go out to the ends of the earth, but also because in the reality of the time, some Christians were legally the property of others.

In addition to the value of work for its own sake, or rather for the sake of glorifying God through the work, work is sanctifying because it results in the earning of money that is to be used to help others, and for the Original Church, this means almsgiving. The consensus of the Church Fathers is that almsgiving is a penance and is expected of all of us (see Tb 4:10; 12:9; Sir 3:30). At least some of what we earn is meant to be used to give alms. As the *Didache* advises, if you earn by the working of your hands, then by those same hands "you shall give a ransom for your sins" (*Didache*, 4:6).

Incidentally, almsgiving, whether giving directly to the poor or giving into the offering plate or poor box in the context of liturgy, was always completely voluntary and up to the discernment of the giver. Granted, the Church did not have administrative costs or building upkeep in the first three centuries of its existence, and even the clergy did not get paid until the third century (being a priest was not a day job). Nevertheless, the point is that the early Church did not continue the Hebrew concept of tithing. All of the many early Christian apologetic and Church order documents (with the possible exception of one) say that giving is voluntary and do not mention tithing. Justin Martyr, in the context of explaining to his pagan audience what Christians do in their worship, wrote, "And those who are well to do, and willing, give what each thinks is appropriate" (*First Apology*, 67). As Tertullian explained it, "On a certain day once a month, each person puts in a small donation, if he so chooses, but only if he wants to, and only if he is able. For there is no compulsion, all is voluntary" (*Apology*, 39). It seems that in Justin's place and time (Rome in the middle of the second century), the collection was taken every week, whereas in Tertullian's place and time (North Africa at the end of the second century), the collection was only received once a month.

MYTH
The Original Church expected Christians to tithe.

TRUTH
Tithing was not an expectation in the Original Church: All giving was voluntary, occasional, and up to the discernment of the giver. Nevertheless, it was considered a penance.

You might be aware that in certain times in the Roman Empire, the government instituted a "dole" in which free bread was handed out to the people, particularly in Rome. However, this was not a welfare system, nor was it a program motivated by compassion. Roman handouts were given according to status, with the wealthiest or highest class lining up first, and often by the time the truly poor got to the front of the line, they had run out of bread. The point of the dole was to make a visible gesture to quiet complaints about the economy, not to actually feed hungry people. It was the appearance that counted, not the actual result. By contrast, Jewish, and therefore Christian, charity was motivated by compassion and a desire to do the will of God and was meant to actually help the poor.

Ultimately, the Original Church taught that those with resources and those without were in a kind of symbiotic relationship. The poor needed the rich, because the rich had money to spare, and it was their ministry to give alms to the poor. But the rich needed the poor as well, since Jesus had made it clear that it is more difficult for the rich to persevere to salvation, and so the rich needed the poor to pray for them. For this reason, almsgiving was, for the most part, not meant to be anonymous. The recipients of the alms needed to know who gave them so that they could pray for their benefactors. In a way, this was an interesting parallel to the traditional Roman patron-client system, in which the wealthy provided benefits to their poorer clients who in turn provided occasional services.

But in spite of this networking and safety net system built into Roman society, the usual custom of the Romans would be to invite to their banquets only those who could invite them back, or repay the favor in some significant way. This is the reason for Jesus's words about inviting to dinner those who cannot repay the invitation, thus feeding those who might otherwise go hungry (Lk 14:12–14). For the Original Church, the way the poor repaid the favor was by their intercession. Notice that the Roman attitude toward banquets was also the problem behind St. Paul's criticisms in 1 Corinthians 11. The apostle was upset with the Christians in Corinth because the wealthy Christians were treating the *agape* meal like a Roman banquet—and this is probably one of the reasons the Sacrament was moved out of the meal and made into a morning liturgy (another reason was probably Roman laws against secret assemblies, making night meetings difficult).

In the early Christian documents, the concept of almsgiving eventually became a catchall that included everything that we would consider the corporal works of mercy. This is because a person could do the works directly or give alms to the Church, and the Church would spend the money on the works of mercy. Justin Martyr continues what he was saying in the quote above:

> And what is collected is given to the presider, who gives aid to the orphans and widows, and those who are in need due to sickness or any other cause, and those who are in prison, and the foreigners sojourning among us, and in a word, takes care of all who are in need. (*First Apology*, 67)

And as Tertullian wrote, the offerings are used

> to support and bury poor people, to supply the needs of poor orphan children, and of old people confined to their houses, and also to anyone who has suffered shipwreck, or are in exile in the islands, or sent to the mines, or locked up in the prisons for nothing but their faithfulness to the cause of God's Church. (*Apology*, 39)

Burial of the dead was especially important in the time of the early Church, since the poor were often in real danger of not getting a proper burial.

The care for the sick was actually one of the primary forms of evangelization in the Original Church. In addition to the martyrdom of Christians, in which their pagan neighbors saw their bravery in the face of death—proof of their belief in a life that is bigger than life—Christians also risked their lives to care for the victims of the many plagues that ravaged the Roman world in the early centuries of Christianity. This was in spite of the fact that superstitious pagans often blamed the Christians for the plagues and for other natural disasters. In fact, the historian Eusebius of Caesarea commented that for a Christian to die as a result of caring for people with contagious illnesses was like a form a martyrdom (*Ecclesiastical History*, 7.22.7–10). Eusebius was actually quoting from a letter written by the bishop Dionysius of Alexandria in the third century, and the passage is worth reproducing here:

> They fearlessly visited the sick, ministering to them in every way, serving them in Christ, and they happily died with them, taking the affliction of others upon themselves, drawing the sickness from their neighbors, and willingly taking on their suffering. And many who cared for the sick and gave strength to others, died themselves, thus transferring their death to themselves. . . . In this manner, truly the best of our brothers departed this life, including some priests and deacons, and people of the highest reputation, so that this form of death, through the great piety and strong faith it exhibited, seemed to be as good as martyrdom. And they took up in their open hands the bodies of the saints and held them to their bosoms, and closed their eyes and their mouths, and carried them on their shoulders and

> laid them out. They would cling to them, embrace them, and prepare them (for burial) by washing and dressing them, and after a little while they received these same services themselves. For the survivors were continually following those who went before them. But with the heathen everything was different. They deserted those who began to get sick, and fled from those dearest to them. And they cast them out into the streets when they were not even dead yet, and the dead they left unburied, like refuse.

The reason I wanted to include this in a chapter on work in the Original Church is to point out that *this*—that is, the works of mercy and almsgiving—is the Original Church's primary form of evangelization. There was no "office" of evangelist in the early Church, other than those bishops, priests, and deacons who read the Gospels in liturgy. But evangelization was the work of every Christian, not by preaching in the streets, but by giving alms and doing the works of mercy in the name of Christ.

The point is that when the Roman Empire was converted to Christianity in the fourth century, it was not simply the actions of the first Christian emperor that converted it. It was the culmination of a long process of conversion which had been going on throughout the whole life of the Church. (Just as the conversion of a person is a process, so is the conversion of an empire.) The emperor Constantine did not convert the empire. The Christian clergy did not convert the empire. The Roman Empire was converted by lay Christians, who simply loved one neighbor at a time, and were willing to give their lives for their faith.

MYTH
Christian preaching is for conversion through apologetics and convincing by logic.

TRUTH
Early Christian preaching was for the people already committed to the Church. The goal of preaching was not to convince people to believe, but to instruct them in their faith. The homily was meant to interpret Scripture and encourage the people to apply it to their lives. Liturgy in the Original Church was not open to visitors, or "seeker-sensitive," or hospitality oriented. Only the baptized received the Eucharist. Evangelization happened outside the worship meeting, wherever Christians lived and worked, through the works of mercy, and by their example, especially in martyrdom.

So, what did Christians in the Original Church actually do for a living? As we have seen, Tertullian and other apologists went out of their way to point out that Christians worked alongside non-Christians in virtually every trade. Christians were represented in almost every profession because the Church was open to everyone and not limited to certain kinds of people. In fact, one of the most common occupations for a Christian in the early Church was as a medical doctor, a profession that was open to both men and women in Roman culture. But there were some occupations that were considered incompatible with the life of a baptized Christian, which meant that people who made a living by these "professions" would be expected to quit their day job before getting baptized. St. Matthew the tax collector was, after all, really St. Matthew the *ex*-tax collector. This is part of the reason why almsgiving was so important in the Original Church—if you had an income, some of your alms were going to feed a family where someone was out of work precisely because they had converted to Christianity.

Some of these incompatible occupations are obvious, like hired assassin, pimp, prostitute, con man, pickpocket, or professional thief (like the guy who steals your clothes while you're in the baths, according to Tertullian, *Apology*, 43–44). And of course, a Christian cannot be the priest or priestess of a pagan cult, which also meant that certain government jobs were off limits, since those jobs required leadership in the cults. Idol makers could keep their trades as sculptors or painters, but had to stop working on the production of idols. And no Christian could be a magus, sorcerer, or dealer in spells and occult objects.

We Have Nothing to Do with the Circus

Among us nothing is ever said, or seen, or heard, which has anything in common with the madness of the circus, the immodesty of the theater, the atrocities of the arena, or the useless exercises of the gymnasium.

–Tertullian, *Apology*, 38

Other prohibited jobs might surprise you. For example, in the quote above, Tertullian speaks for the consensus of the apologists and early theologians when he says that there is something inherently sinful in what were called the "spectacles" of the Roman shows. The circus was the oval horserace track, but a day's shows also included public executions. In the arena, gladiators fought—not always to the death, but the point was that real death and dismemberment were entertainment. In the theaters, many of the plays were basically live sex shows, the ancient world's equivalent of watching porn. And in the gymnasia of the bath complexes, men wrestled in the nude (the word *gymnasium* literally means "the naked room").

In all of these cases, the shows were dedicated to the pagan gods and were accompanied by pagan rituals. Any deaths were, for all intents and purposes, human sacrifices to the pagan gods. And the circuses, arenas, and theaters were all surrounded by brothels, had vendors selling spells and potions, and had prostitutes standing in the archways under the bleachers. In fact, the Latin word for the archway, the *fornix*, is where we get our English word "fornication." And so, we have several documents from the early Church with titles like *On the Spectacles*. In these documents, apologists and theologians decry the sinfulness of the shows and explain in no uncertain terms that real Christians do not go to the circus, arena, or theater. But, to quote Shakespeare, "Methinks [they] doth protest too much." In other words, what we get in those documents may be more the ideal than the reality; more of a sermon meant for people who *did* go to the shows, to try to shame them into not going.

Some of the apologists and theologians explicitly say that to *watch* something sinful is as much of a sin as to participate in it. So, if you watch a man die in the arena, you have willingly participated in his murder and committed a mortal sin. If you watch a live sex show in the theater, you have willingly participated in adultery. I think there are good reasons for believing this is theologically correct and still true today, but the ongoing recurrence of documents like this from the time of the early Church presents us with a reality that was a bit messy. One theologian even complained that Christians were receiving the Eucharist, and while the Body and Blood of Christ were still within them, taking them right to the shows, or worse, to a brothel (Novatian, *On the Spectacles*, 5.5). Culturally, it might have been a little bit like a preacher telling his congregation that football is a sin, knowing all the while that they are checking their watches to make sure they don't miss the kickoff.

The point for our purposes here is that jobs associated with the shows were considered unsuitable for a baptized Christian. Actors were seen as people who sell their bodies—they put their bodies on display, and so made their living by immodesty, or worse, by a form of prostitution. Obviously, the live sex shows were a form of prostitution, not to mention adultery. And in all but the live sex shows, female roles were often played by men, which was seen as a form of transvestitism. Even among the wider Roman culture, actors were considered untrustworthy because they were good liars—they could take on a false identity and make it convincing. For Tertullian, actors (and gladiators) sacrificed their bodies on a stage dedicated to pagan gods, which was as good as offering themselves as a sacrifice to those idols. For the same reasons, gladiators, gladiator trainers, and even charioteers would be expected to find new kinds of work if they desired Christian baptism.

Some jobs were debated as to their fitness for the Christian. One debate that was never really settled was whether a teacher, once baptized, could continue teaching secular literature. "Secular" in this context means pagan—so could a Christian teach the classical literature of the old Greco-Roman myths (like Homer or Virgil), or would that be a participation in paganism? Some said they should give up the old books, but others said it was acceptable to read and even teach them, as long as they didn't believe that the stories were true.

Another debated profession was soldier. Could a Christian continue to serve in the legions? An early layer of the *Apostolic Tradition* seems to imply that someone who is already a soldier and converts may continue to be a soldier, but that a baptized Christian should not join up if he is not already in the military. The author of this Church order manual (Hippolytus?) wrote that it is acceptable to be a soldier, but a Christian soldier may not execute anyone. If followed, this stipulation would prevent one's rise in the ranks, since it was inevitable that at a certain level of rank there would at least be the expectation of ordering corporal punishment and torture, if not execution. For the same reason, certain government jobs were out of bounds because those jobs required oversight of the arrest, torture, and execution of prisoners (the Original Church was generally opposed to capital punishment). What this meant was that a Christian man was at least limited, if not prevented, from following the traditional Roman *cursus honorum*, the career track of upward mobility from the military into politics.

The question of Christian soldiers was finally settled when the emperor Constantine attended the regional Council of Arles in the year 314 (the first time an emperor attended a Christian council, even before the Council of Nicaea). Since by then the hope was that someday all Romans would also be Christians, it became clear very quickly that to prevent Christians from serving in the military would leave the empire with no legions. No doubt the example of the many soldier saints like St. Sebastian also helped in the discernment of that decision.

We can see that, with the exception of a few occupations that were considered inherently sinful, Christians worked their jobs like anyone else, except perhaps more joyfully and without the bitterness of feeling that came from the belief that they were unfortunate simply because they had to work. But they did not see themselves as distinct from non-Christians because of their work, and—this is important— *they did not make their work a distinguishing factor in their Christian identity*.

What was far more important to them was their sense of vocation. To be clear, occupation and vocation are not the same thing. Your occupation is what puts food on the table (though it does also facilitate the giving of alms). But your *vocation* has to do with the sacraments, and sacramental vows. For the Original Christians, their identity was not based on their place in the world, but on their place in the Church. Their primary identity was that they were members in the family of God, having been baptized, and then after that, whatever other sacramental vows they had taken, such as holy orders or holy matrimony. For most of the Original

Christians, it was marriage and family. In fact, the Church rejected several heresies that proposed that all Christians should be celibate.

In general, I think it's fair to say that the primary vocation of a Christian, then as now, is to be intentional about our personal holiness, and to facilitate and encourage the sanctification of others. For those of us who are called to the vocation of matrimony, that means serving our spouses and actively working to enable their sanctification and the sanctification of our children. A person's occupation does not define his or her identity, but the occupation pays the bills to make the vocation possible. Work is sanctifying, in part, because it makes family, and the works of mercy, possible.

It's worth clarifying at this point that in the Original Church, no one saw the Christian identity or vocation as having anything to do with "fighting injustice." To some extent, this is because the Church was an illegal and persecuted religion for a very long time, and it existed as a marginalized minority in an empire that did not value the individual (most individuals were considered expendable). Therefore, very few people thought of themselves as having any ability to "change the world." Don't get me wrong, it's good to oppose injustice and to improve the lives of people as an expression of the gospel. In truth, the early Christians did fight injustice by taking an adamant pro-life stance, and by backing that up with their actions when they rescued and adopted discarded babies. They also fought injustice by refusing to participate in the predatory systems of institutionalized child abuse disguised as mentoring or tutoring. And they did improve the lives of people when they cared for the sick.

But they didn't worry about "systemic injustice" as if they could convert the culture, because they recognized that salvation is not salvation from injustice but rather salvation from sin. Or to put it another way, they understood that people need to be saved from their own sins, not from somebody else's. The Original Christians recognized that freedom is not the personal freedom to do whatever you want, but freedom from sin; it's the spiritual freedom to conform your will to the will of God.

And so, they *did* convert the culture. But they didn't do it by trying to make the world a better place; they did it by trying to make people better and more fit for eternity. They didn't do it by making people more comfortable; they did it by making people more holy. When they prayed, "Thy kingdom come," they knew it was not up to them to build the kingdom on earth, but rather they prayed for God's eternal kingdom to be revealed. They meant this in the sense of that Aramaic phrase, *marana tha*, "Our Lord, come [soon]" (1 Cor 16:22). And ironically, they *did* change the world, because they were not trying to change the world. They didn't change the world by changing "systems"; they changed the world by changing hearts. They converted the empire by loving one neighbor at a time.

The point is that the vocation of a Christian is to make ourselves holy, and to help others make themselves holy. It is not to change the world to accommodate us, but to change ourselves to accommodate ourselves to the kingdom. But again, that does change the world, one person at a time. And when the empire came to be converted to Christianity, the Church did eventually have the influence to conform the culture to the morality of the Faith. Eventually they got rid of the blood sports and almost got rid of slavery (it came back with a vengeance in the late Middle Ages, but after the popes had condemned it). The point is that the work of the Christian is not to change the world, especially if that becomes a distraction that allows us to tolerate or justify actual personal sin. God will change the world in his own good time, one way or another. The vocation of the Christian is to change people through the works of mercy.

So, what does all this mean for us as Christians in the twenty-first century? Like many people today, Roman elites did not consider work to be dignified. The wealthiest 1 to 3 percent in the empire made their living by owning land, which was inherited or given to them by the emperors as rewards for their service. These wealthy landowners either had a large number of slaves to work the land, or they rented out the land to be farmed by tenants. But the rest of the

97 to 99 percent worked hard, sunup to sundown, seven days a week. There would be no official day of rest until Christianity was legalized in the fourth century and the new Christian emperor, Constantine, made Sunday a holiday. In a sense, he invented the weekend, but of course it was for the purpose of setting aside a new Christian Sabbath—honoring the day already designated by the Church as the primary day for worship. And it must be said that in our own time, keeping the Sabbath holy is one of the easiest commandments to forget, and break, and yet it is a great witness to our neighbors when we do it.

In any case, the difference between a Christian who works and a non-Christian who works is not in the work itself, but in their attitude toward work. The pagan bemoans his fate as someone who is unfortunate because he has to work. The Christian approaches work as something given to him by God, for the purpose of supporting a family and for almsgiving. Jesus worked. The apostles worked. Why should disciples of Jesus and imitators of the apostles feel entitled not to work?

In some ways, though, this entitlement of the wealthy not to have to work not only still exists today, but in fact it has spread to those who are not wealthy. There is an epidemic of thinking that somehow having to work hard means we are the victim of an injustice. You may have heard a motivational speaker say something to this effect: "Figure out what you love to do, then find a way to do that for a living, and you'll never work a day in your life."'I think that this is an extremely irresponsible thing to say, especially to youth and young adults, not only because it perpetuates the idea that somehow work is undignified and should be avoided, but also because life simply doesn't work that way. It's no different from saying, "Figure out how much money you want, then find a way to get it, and you'll never work a day in your life." No kidding.

Most people do not get to do what they love for a living, and that's normal. The problem is when young people feel as though they are entitled to a day job that's fun, and then feel like they have failed in life if they can't make that false promise work, if they have to do something they don't particularly enjoy in order to support a family. Many feel that if they have to work a whole regular work week, if they have to be at work more waking hours than they get to play, they have somehow fallen into a pitiful state.

Most early Christians, like their unbelieving neighbors, did not imagine what they would be when they grew up, or went to college and majored in something. They fell into an apprenticeship, or they scraped together a living by buying and selling, or they did domestic work in their own, or other people's, houses. They tried to bloom where they were planted and they saw their income, such as it was, as God's providence. They prayed for God to bless their work, but they did not make their day job into their identity. Far more important to them was their sacramental vocation. For the average lay Christians in the Original Church, their identity was first and foremost their place in the Church as an extended family, and second, their place in their own family. Their identity was not their job, trade, or skill set, because then, as now, these were easily lost—and then what happens to a person's identity, if his identity is wrapped up in his job, and he loses his job? No, work was not a "passion," or even a source of pride. Work was holy, not for its own sake, but because it sanctifies (the more so if it's a source of suffering) and because it pays the bills and allows one to do the really important things, like support a family and give alms (including the support of those in religious orders and communities). The occupation exists to pay for the vocation. We work so that we can share. We work for the benefit of others.

This means that, on the one hand, we need our identity to be detached from our day job enough that we are ready to quit that job if it ever becomes a hindrance to our sanctification. The early Christians knew that some jobs were incompatible with the Faith, and they were much less tolerant of "gray areas" than we usually are today. In our time, we may need to bring back the conversation about whether there are some jobs that a Christian should not do. At the very least, everyone who earns a wage should ask that question of themselves, and not compartmentalize the job as if simply the need for a paycheck justifies anything. And this also means that we need to be ready to support those who, for reasons of their own (and their family's) sanctification and salvation, discern that they must quit a job.

It's also worth reminding ourselves that in the Original Church, being a bishop, priest, or deacon was not a day job that came with a salary. That didn't happen until the third century at the earliest. And up until the fourth century, clergy were often married men who also had to support a family. The Western Church developed to require celibacy of clergy in the fourth century, and for good reasons—not least is that it turned out to be very difficult for one person to fulfill both vocations of priesthood and matrimony (1 Cor 7:7–18)—but the point here is that in the Original Church, the division between clergy and laity was not a division according to occupation, as if clergy worked a different (or higher, more spiritual) job. Clergy had their sacramental vocation of holy orders, but they also worked a day job like everyone else. This means that often the laity had a healthier sense of the dignity and sanctifying effect of ordinary labor than laypeople do now, simply because they were not tempted to see their occupations as "less" than that of the clergy. They recognized the universal call to holiness in the realm of work. Or, at least, I think they did. I can't prove it, since they didn't write down their thoughts for us to read, but even if I'm wrong, we can recapture some of that ideal if we choose to.

But this also means that the tasks of ministry were not so often relegated only to the clergy as they are today. Lay Christians participated in the works of mercy and, in fact, this was the Original Church's evangelization. That and martyrdom. The evangelists of the early Church were the lay Christians who fed the hungry, cared for the sick, and gave their lives for the Faith.

MYTH
The celibacy of clergy was an invention of the Middle Ages, to prevent the sons of clergy from inheriting their fathers' positions or land.

TRUTH
Clergy celibacy developed in the West in the fourth century, in part on the assumption that all Christians should abstain from marital intimacy for twenty-four hours before receiving the Eucharist, and yet a bishop or priest must be ready to preside over the sacrament every day.

Finally, a word on what we do outside of work, with our free time. The early Christians didn't have much time for hobbies. For the most part, the pursuit of "passions" was a luxury of the rich. What Roman society did offer them, the games and shows, was a temptation. In the "spectacles," human misery was on display, and the degradation and exploitation of human life was entertainment. I daresay we now live in a world where this is once again the case. Social media, the gossip culture, and reality television all do for the twenty-first century person what the games and shows of ancient Rome did for the Romans, which is provide distractions from life in the form of drama, controversy, and schadenfreude. But as the Church Fathers pointed out, we cannot be entertained by these things without participating in what causes suffering to others (even if they are willing participants). In other words, we cannot participate in something that has the opposite effect of our vocation—that is, that works against the sanctification of others. If we *work* for the benefit of others, we cannot *play* in a way that is to their detriment.

CHAPTER SIX

We Are Laughed At

We are laughed at for proclaiming that God will one day judge the world. . . . If you think [Christians are absurd], let them be absurd, for they are still useful, since they make of all who believe them better men and women, if only from the fear of eternal punishment and the hope of eternal bliss.

–Tertullian, *Apology*, 47, 49

In the time of the Original Church, faithful Christianity was marginalized and often persecuted. Christians were accused of being antisocial, ridiculed as unenlightened, oppressed by religious discrimination, and persecuted on a variety of trumped-up charges from arson to treason. But they were willing to break the law to practice their faith, and by their faithfulness, they converted the empire to the point that the empire would eventually take up their morals, virtues, and teachings as its own. Some of us are old enough to remember when the effects of that conversion—even though so many centuries before—could still be felt in our own culture. But those days are over. The time when parents could send their children to public school and count on them absorbing traditional Judeo-Christian values is gone, and this is true in more and more places.

This example is just one of the many pieces of evidence that tell us that we have come full circle, to the point where to be a faithful Catholic is to be countercultural and to live as a stranger in the world. It is as Jesus predicted it would be. Citizens of the kingdom must live as foreigners in the world—ambassadors of the kingdom, to be sure, but still foreigners. And those who hold on to ancient values, traditions, and teachings will increasingly be considered dangerous to society by those who value change above everything else and who make themselves and their desires their own highest authority.

It is perhaps the greatest irony that those who oppose perversion are being called perverted by those who wish to justify their perversion. But it's nothing new—in fact, it is old. It is original. And that irony was not lost on the early Christian apologists. It drove the often sarcastic tone of their writings. Nevertheless, this is why it was so important to the Church Fathers to make sure that new converts understood what they were signing up for before being baptized. But it was not hard to get new converts to take their responsibilities seriously, since most of them had seen Christians die for the Faith, and they knew that was on the table. They might have to give their lives. So, what can we learn from the Original Church about how to live as faithful Catholics? How might we be asked to "give our lives," as in, dedicate our very lifestyles in radical ways of living counter-culturally?

You Can Kill Us, but You Cannot Hurt Us

As for us, we believe that no evil can be done to us. . . . You can kill us, but not hurt us.

–St. Justin Martyr, *First Apology*, 2

It should go without saying that we are called to pursue the same holiness as the Original Christians. And if we can assume that there are ways in which we can imitate the early Christians, or at least take a page from their way of life, we have to begin by acknowledging that part of our goal is to strike a balance between really living our identity as members of the Body of Christ on the one hand, and yet living in the world and for the benefit of the world on the other. This is that balance, often stated as a paraphrase of John 15:19, to be "in the world, but not *of* the world." What Jesus actually says in that verse is, "If you belonged to the world, the world would love you as its own. Because you do not belong to the world, but I have chosen you out of the world—therefore the world hates you."

For most of us, especially those of us who are lay Catholics, called to the vocation of holy matrimony and the family, our life is not to be cloistered. By our vocation, we don't keep ourselves apart from the world and, in fact, we try to raise our children to be ready to go out of our homes and into the world, hopefully to make their own families as new cells in the Body of Christ. And so, we are—and must be— like the early Christians: The world opposed them, but they didn't circle the wagons, they lived and worked in the world, and to the extent that they could without seeking after danger, they didn't keep their faith private. Like them, we cannot afford to be so private about our faith that our neighbors don't even know we're Catholic. There is a reason why we make the Sign of the Cross on our bodies. It's not just for us, it's for those who see it, and by it we identify ourselves as Christians.

On the other hand, the Original Christians did not let the world convert them. Since the family (and the home) is the basic cell of the Body of Christ, there is a sense in which it is essential to keep the world out of our homes. Our homes have to be a place of refuge from the world, in which the sanctification of the family is facilitated. Some have even made the case that the Catholic home must be a kind of domestic monastery.

To that end, and for the sake of helping readers synthesize what we've explored in this book, I want to end by presenting a kind of "rule" for the domestic "monastery" of the home. What follows is a summary of this book, to help you think about applying what you've read in everyday life, to sanctify your life and work. To be clear, this is for lay Catholics and other Christians—not just clergy or professional theologians. This is not some method for a "higher tier" of spirituality; I would argue these are the basics for all believers. You don't have to be ordained or have an advanced degree to fulfill your vocation as a disciple of Jesus Christ.

What this means, though, is that it is more important than ever for the lay Catholic to have a strong sense of identity. We have to be clear about how we are different from the rest of the culture if we are to live counter-culturally and be faithful to the religion that we have received. Therefore, you will remember that we began by saying that the Original Church defined Christian identity on four levels: membership in the Church as a family, faithfulness to what we have received, commitment to Christian morality, and a rightly ordered approach to work. These will provide the framework, or the scaffolding, on which we will build our "rule."

The Blood of Christians Is Seed

We conquer by dying. . . . Your cruelty, no matter how extreme, does not do anything for you. . . . The more you mow us down, the more we grow in number. The blood of Christians is seed. . . . For who could contemplate this, and not be excited to inquire what is at the bottom of it? Who could inquire about it, and not embrace our doctrines? And once he has embraced them, who would not desire to suffer, that he may become partaker of the fulness of God's grace, that he may obtain from God complete forgiveness, by giving his blood in exchange? For that secures the remission of all offences. And this is why it is that we thank you, on the spot, for your condemnations. . . . When we are condemned by you, we are acquitted by the Most High.

–Tertullian, *Apology*, 50

A Rule for a Household: A Cell in the Body of Christ

Based on the Life of Lay Catholics in the Original Church

We Live as Members in a Family

1. We belong to something that is greater than ourselves. We are not alone in life. We need the family of the Church, and the sacraments, to help us in the process of sanctification.
2. We submit to that to which we belong. We are not our own highest authority, but we recognize and respect the order within the family that is the Church. We have let go of the idea that by our own reason we get to decide what is true and what is false, but rather we admit that we must receive truth from God's revelation, handed down to us through the Tradition of the Church.
3. We consider our parish as an extension of our family, and we are committed to our participation in it as an important part of our lifestyle. We set an example for our

children by making Mass and holy days priorities, and by attending to our own spirituality.

4. We prioritize the Body of Christ as our primary family, and we are careful not to spend time with people, not even with relatives, who present us with temptations or are negative influences on our children.
5. We teach our children that they, too, are a part of something greater than themselves, and greater than their immediate family; something worldwide and timeless.

We Believe What We Have Received

1. We Believe in the Trinity
    - We accept the teachings of the Church, to whatever extent we understand them, and we do not presume to know better than the Tradition what is true.
    - We make an effort to learn what the Church teaches, and to understand the meaning of the creeds, according to our ability.
    - We read the Scriptures, including all of the books in the Catholic Bible, which was the Bible of Jesus and the apostles. We acknowledge that we need the Tradition of the Church to help us interpret and understand the Scriptures.
    - We teach these things to our children, and help them understand why we believe what we believe.

- We make the Sign of the Cross often, and in public, as a witness to our Catholic Christian identity and faith.

2. We Believe in the Eucharist
   - We are uncompromising in our belief in the Real Presence of the Body and Blood of Christ in the Eucharist.
   - We receive the sacrament of the Eucharist at least weekly, and we acknowledge that regular reception of the Eucharist is required for the ongoing connection to Jesus Christ that leads us to salvation.
   - We keep the Sabbath; that is, we set aside Sundays (including the vigil) for Mass and family time, for the sake of our own peace and holiness, but also as a witness to the world of our identity and faith.
3. We Believe in the Communion of the Saints
   - We prioritize eternity, or seek first the kingdom, by keeping our perspective on the "big picture"—that life is not limited to the present, earthly life.
   - We celebrate the feasts of the saints and make of our lives a rhythm of feasting and fasting that sanctifies even our very calendars.
   - We make an effort to take time to stand on holy ground, by visiting the graves of our loved ones or making pilgrimages to holy sites or local shrines. We

pray in the presence of the relics of the saints, and we ask for the intercession of the saints.

- We do not settle for funeral home or secular memorial services for our Catholic loved ones, but we send them off with funeral Masses held in Catholic churches. We do not spread their ashes in places that are not consecrated ground.
- We teach our children that they, too, live within the stream of the Faith, receiving it from their ancestors and handing it on to their spiritual descendants. We are conscious of all those who come after us in the Faith and that we are in some small way handing on the Faith to them.

We are Committed to the Ideals of Christian Morality

1. We do not trade the ideals of traditional morality for conformity with progress or changes in society; the goal of the Church is not social transformation but rather the conversion of hearts to conformity with Jesus Christ.
2. We are uncompromisingly pro-life, and we support pro-life causes and ministries. In our marriages, we are open to life. We support adoption as the alternative to abortion.
3. We protect children from corruption, even when it comes from threats that are now legal in our society. We are aware that, depending on where we live, we may not be able to trust our children to public schools, and

in any case, we prefer Catholic schools; where it is not impossible, we make it a priority (even financially) to send our children to Catholic schools.

4. We keep and affirm the distinction between civil marriage and the sacrament of holy matrimony; the latter being a sacred vocation, which has as its goal the sanctification of the couple and the household.
5. We reject all forms of the occult, including horoscopes, tarot cards, psychics, and the like. We keep our homes pure of occult paraphernalia. We also keep our lives and homes pure of all pornography.

We Sanctify the World Through Our Work

1. We do not build our identity on the foundation of our occupations. We do not define ourselves by our jobs, and we recognize that there are times when a Catholic must leave a job that includes expectations of immoral practices, compromises the Faith, presents serious temptation, or comes to be in competition with Church and/or family.
2. We recognize the difference between occupation and vocation, and we prioritize vocations that are associated with the sacraments, especially (for the lay Catholic) holy matrimony, family, and children.
3. We embrace work as having a purpose other than the job itself, which is to make vocation possible—that is,

to give us an income that pays for home and family, almsgiving, and participation in the works of mercy.

4. We financially support those with other vocations, including clergy and those in religious orders and communities.
5. In our free time, we avoid the "spectacles"—that is, we avoid all forms of entertainment that rely on other people's suffering or exploitation. We reject pornography, and we intentionally consider and discern whether to be spectators of forms of entertainment that result in injury or humiliation of anyone (even if they are willing participants).
6. We are not ashamed of our Catholic Faith; it is not private. We live our faith in the world, as a witness to the world, yet we do not seek or engage in controversy. Evangelization is not primarily done through apologetics, but through introducing people to Jesus Christ and inviting them into his family.
7. We do not change the world by trying to change the world; we change the world by loving one neighbor at a time—that is, by changing hearts. (If you want to rid the world of "systemic injustice" or "corporate sin," you'll have to befriend the CEO or some other people with the power to change things and share the Faith with them.)
8. We look for ways to feed the hungry. (Could the Church revive the *agape* meal as a combination potluck and soup

kitchen or food pantry? What if ours were not one or the other, with the members of the parish sharing their food with each other but only separately feeding the hungry with donated food? What if the hungry were invited in to where they could meet and interact with people from the parish? And what if, as the early Christians did, we sent the leftovers out to the shut-ins? What if *that* was our "church growth" program—inviting people into the family by the works of mercy?)

To Go Deeper: Other Books by the Author

Reading the Church Fathers: A History of the Early Church and the Development of Doctrine
Contains all the background information for everything I've talked about here. All of the writers of the Original Church quoted in the present book are introduced, along with their writings. Includes detailed footnotes with references to primary sources. Overall, this is the story of the early Church with all the historical context.

Praying Like the Early Church: Seven Insights from the Church Fathers to Help You Connect with God
How did lay Christians in the Original Church pray? What did their devotional lives look like? These questions are answered along with more on the lived practice of the Faith in the early Church. The companion volume is *Praying the Psalms: The Divine Gateway to Lectio Divina and Contemplative Prayer*.

Reading Scripture Like the Early Church: Seven Insights from the Church Fathers to Help You Understand the Bible

How did the Original Christians read and interpret Scripture? Did they read it "literally"? This includes examples and outlines the method of early Christian interpretation in a way that makes it easy to try it for yourself.

How Christianity Saved Civilization . . . and Must Do So Again

Cowritten with Mike Aquilina, this is the book that started it all. Here we outline the ways in which the Church in our culture has come full circle, back to a position of being marginalized, forcing the Church to embrace its countercultural place in society.

Handed Down: The Catholic Faith of the Early Christians

This book goes into more detail on the differences between Catholic doctrine and Protestant thought, including concepts such as *sola Scriptura* (Scripture and Tradition) and *sola fide*, (faith and works), and it includes an in-depth chapter on early and medieval Christian Eucharistic theology.

What Really Happens After We Die: How We Know There Will Be Hugs in Heaven!

This book is about the doctrine of the resurrection, especially as we receive it from the Church Fathers. It outlines the Original Church's teachings on death, purgatory, heaven, and the general resurrection.

A Week in the Life of Rome

This is historical fiction, with info boxes meant to help the reader understand the life of the Original Church in the context of the Roman Empire. The story takes place in the year AD 50, in the city of Rome, and includes several characters mentioned in the New Testament, including St. Peter.